Confronting Popular Cults

M. Thomas Starkes

BROADMAN PRESS
Nashville, Tennessee

Dewey Decimal Classification Number: 290
Library of Congress catalog card number: 72–79177
Printed in the United States of America

Contents

ALTERNATIVES TO DISCIPLESHIP

Astrology has become a major religious concern in the Western world. It is a $210-million annual business in the United States, with one New York company alone turning out more than a thousand computerized horoscopes daily. Martin E. Marty, church historian and observer of the contemporary religious scene in America, offers this analysis of astrology:

> As fun and games, who cares? As alternative religion, I care. . . . I want to preserve at least enough inconoclastic sense to shatter idols and to desacralize sanctuaries and to see whether freedom in Christ just might help overcome some of the "elemental spirits" that the gospel of Jesus Christ set out to counter.[1]

Minority religions have been branded and castigated for generations by well-meaning critics. Mostly, they have been placed under the general headings of "cults" and many of the basic textbooks in the area such as *The Chaos of Cults*[2] have used this term to refer to such groups as Mormons, Jehovah's Witnesses, and Christian Scientists.

The term "sect" is used by some who group religious movements according to sociological standards. For Ernst Troeltsch, the characteristics of the sects include emphasis on lay Christianity, indifference toward the authority of the state, directness of the personal religious relationship, criticism of official spiritual guides and theologians, and the appeal to the New

Testament and the primitive church.[3] Even casual observers
will note immediately that these characteristics also apply to
some evangelical Christian groups such as Southern Baptists.
Therefore, the term is also an inaccurate word to describe
the minority religious groups in America such as the Black
Muslims.

The groups commonly called cults or sects have in common a deviant theology, especially in regard to authority.
Horton Davies, speaking of his choice for a title of a book,
wrote:

> The title, *Christian Deviations,* is the best I can devise to cover
> a highly varied and selected group of new movements . . .
> Christian Science, Mormonism, and Jehovah's Witnesses, since all
> have added other special sources of revelation to the Bible and, to
> that extent, modified its primary authority, are adequately covered
> by the present title.[4]

Three examples of the way the groups being discussed here
view God suffice to show how they have deviated from Christian thought. Jehovah's Witnesses say, for example, that
God's Holy Spirit is *not* a God, not a member of a trinity,
not coequal with Jehovah and is not a person. For Christian
Scientists, life, truth, and love constitute the triune person
called God, the father-mother. Christ is the spiritual idea of
sonship, divine science, or the holy comforter. Deviation from
Christian thought is evident in these viewpoints.

The central issue in the comparison of religious groups is
that of authority, i.e., where one goes to decide what he is
to do and believe. Each of the groups discussed in this book
do radically alter Christian sources of authority such as the
Bible and the role of Jesus Christ. For that reason, they can
legitimately be called Christian deviations.

However, religious experience includes more than search
for authority. H. Richard Niebuhr made this discovery a half
century ago while trying to approach the problem of church

unity from a purely theological point of view. He wrote that theological opinions have their roots in the relationship of the religious life to the cultural and political conditions prevailing in any group of Christians. He concluded:

Where theology is regarded only from the ideological point of view, sight is lost of those very conditions which influence the divergence of its forms, and differences are explained on a speciously intellectual basis without taking into account the fundamental reasons for such variations. [5]

For the Unitarian-Universalist, religion is basically a combination of philosophical pursuit and social concern, evidenced by such discussion topics as, "The United Nations and the Question of Two Chinas." For the Black Muslim, religious life is a combination of Islam, Christianity, and a negative reaction to the "white" Christianity he has encountered. These examples suffice here to demonstrate that religious experience is more than theology or doctrinal deviation from mainstream Christian thought.

Viewed from the perspective of evangelical Christianity, with emphasis on the twin authorities of Jesus as living Word and the Bible as written Word, these groups form a major concern. They are alternatives to discipleship in the sense of constituting threats to Christian discipleship as pictured in the New Testament. Properly understood, that discipleship displays the following characteristics:

1. It is under the complete lordship of Christ, viewing him as the eternally divine criterion by which action and belief are to be judged.
2. It is world-affirming, i.e., true discipleship is not an escape from kingdom building in this present age.
3. True discipleship takes Christ's words seriously when he consistently placed service to and respect for humans above sets of religious laws.

4. This discipleship lives in the strength of personal relationship with the physically resurrected Lord through the continuing presence of the Holy Spirit.
5. True discipleship recognizes that truth, wherever it is found, sets one free. It also acts on the basis that the Christ-event is God's highest and clearest revelation of himself.
6. True discipleship is built on a serious view of the Scriptures with interest in allowing them to speak thematically for themselves with no superimposed scheme over them.

The description above is a common view of Christian discipleship agreed to by most Christians. Alternate forms of discipleship tend to divert persons from following Christ in world-changing service. Together, they constitute a serious threat and challenge to more traditional forms of Christianity. For that reason, they are considered here.

The respective groups discussed herein form varying challenges to discipleship. Zen Buddhism speaks primarily to a youth subculture down on materialism and up on meditation and celebration. British-Israelism appeals to a specific type of patriotism which sees the United States and England as chosen nations. Together, they attract millions away from following Christ in active service and worship.

Evangelical Christians frequently have had to struggle for religious toleration and liberty. They should be the last to deny that precious freedom to others. The alternatives to discipleship are part of the human search for legitimate religious concerns. Man is incurably religious. He develops a life-style or philosophy of life which makes some judgments about the fundamental questions of who or what is God, man, and society. Man also operates on some thought pattern of what the future world after death holds for him. Many persons severely alter their lives on the basis of what they think the next world holds. The experience of religion is universal. Man is basically a believer. He worships, whether it be ancestors or a new home. He prays, whether it be in a Pentecostal faith-healing meeting or in some appeal to superstition. His right to do so must not be denied by those who are evangelical Christians.

Reasons for Rapid Growth

In an open market for truth, where alternatives to discipleship are free to make their claims attractive to an open society, they are bound to attract a few followers. However, the rapid growth of some groups is alarming to evangelical Christians. The Latter-Day Saints grew by 10 percent in the years between 1955 and 1965 to a current national membership of 1.9 million. Jehovah's Witnesses now boast an American membership of four hundred thousand. Black Muslims have been the most consistently growing manifestation of "Black Power" since 1929 with a current hard-core membership of one-quarter million.

The reasons for rapid growth among these alternatives to discipleship are many and complex. However, some patterns do emerge. J. K. Van Baalen established the thesis that the rise of the alternative groups to such a dominant force on the American religious scene should serve as an impetus for renewal within more established denominations. He said the "cults" are a result of "the unpaid bills of the churches." Horton Davies phrased the same sentiment more positively when he stated that these minority religions should stand as a "summons to reformation" to the church.[6] Whatever the terminology, the fact is clear that the emergence of the Christian deviations is at least partially due to the neglect among evangelical Christians of "the edifying of the body of Christ" mentioned in Ephesians 4:12 and 1 Timothy 1:4. This may best be termed as the sin of neglect.

One example of neglect is that in the field of economics. A world-affirming discipleship should produce such active Christian concern that few people would ever be in a position of economic despair. The Jehovah's Witnesses have been described frequently as composed of the bitter from whom life has stolen hope, the malcontent who are eaten up with disgust at the present world system, the simple, the illiterate, the dejected, and the underprivileged. Those are the very persons with whom Jesus spent much of his earthly ministry. More reactionary than a subculture, the Jehovah's Witnesses are part of a contraculture in which the conflict motif is central. The Witness values are conscious contradictions of the values of society's dominant culture, as in the case of failure to salute the flag. The Witnesses are made up predominantly of those people whom society has forgotten. Unfortunately, so have some evangelical Christians and their churches.

Werner Stark reminds the reader that there exists in every upper class (economically) an almost invisible group which shares one decisive feature with the lower classes even though it may share no others with them: the feeling of unhappiness.[7] These unhappy persons form a group to which evangelical Christians can minister.

The luxury of unconcern about the discontent in our society is no longer possible. The rapid growth of the alternative groups make the following statement true in the present tense: "For the thousands who demand answers and hope and are circling around the traditional church with unpleasant questions, the theologian slams the door. . . . And so the disenchanted wanderer moves on, finding his answer in some cultic deviation."[8] Hopefully, this will not be an accurate statement in the future, when evangelical Christians desert a "middle-class" ministry aimed primarily at their own kind.

The Black Muslims stand as a reminder of the failure of

some evangelical Christians to be converted to man as well as to God. The group is an expression of the growing restlessness of a people in search of a social identity, a break from imitating white religion. As such, the Black Muslims are a challenge to evangelical Christians to face such pertinent facts that Elijah Muhammad was born Elijah Poole in Sandersville, Georgia—the son of a Baptist minister.

Some alternative groups spotlight the role of women in their service. Mary Baker Eddy founded Christian Science; Emma Hale Smith was prominent in the beginning of the Reorganized Church of Jesus Christ of Latter-Day Saints; black women are highly respected by the Black Muslims; some prominent female leaders such as Susan B. Anthony were active Unitarians. Women play prominent roles on the current scene in some of these groups under discussion. More than two thirds of the official Christian Science practitioners are women.

Neglect by evangelical churches which has given rise to the alternative to discipleship groups includes not only social groupings but aspects of the personality. The first aspect of the personality too frequently neglected is the mind. Carl F. H. Henry, former editor of the popular magazine *Christianity Today,* has said frequently that the greatest danger evangelical Christians face is anti-intellectualism. Brilliant young evangelical doctors and other professional persons have been attracted to Unitarianism, with their emphasis on the free and open search for intellectual truth. They listen with ready ears to advocates of a religion which sees as its primary function the nurturing of reason. Simplistic statements, such as "it makes no difference what you believe in your mind; it's what you believe in your heart that really matters," will not suffice in evangelical churches where more and more masters and doctoral degrees are evident.

Another aspect of the personality which is at times neglected is that of emotional maturity. In an age of anxiety, psychological and emotional health must be of major concern to all churches. Christian Science, with its practitioners and genuine interest in peace of mind, exercises a constant ministry to those seeking positive affirmation of their own lives. When ministry to the whole man includes the emotions, growth in the mind-healing groups will level off.

A third area of neglect in the category of personality makeup is that of the body. This area of "applied Christianity," i.e., getting the connection between belief and practice, is evidenced by such groups as Jehovah's Witnesses, who spend long hours in door-to-door witnessing. Jesus spent a good measure of his time talking of and demonstrating ministry to the total physical needs of man.

A fourth area of the personality which needs ministry is the spirit. The personal piety which has characterized evangelical Christians needs reemphasis. Verbal witnessing flows from an up-to-date life in the Spirit coupled with a disciplined program of Bible study and memorization. Devotional life aids in preparation of the spirit for coping adequately with alternatives to discipleship.

Search for the Unusual

The early 1970's were a severely critical set of years in which alienation became a way of saying that man was removed from God and from his fellowman. There was an accompanying loss of confidence in scientism as a way of removing such social ills as war, poverty, and racial hatred.

In the middle of all this turmoil, some forms of religion seemed to be devoid of feeling. Some were looking for consolation. Paul R. Clifford summarized the feelings of many:

The fact is that most people do not feel that the church really meets them in either its teaching or its ritual. . . . The Christian gospel is not addressed to the surface of life, to its conventionalities and its pretenses. . . . Unless it breaks through to the inner springs of human nature and awakens the profoundest emotional response, it will obviously appear to be a hollow sham.[9]

Due to what some would call a lack of feeling in evangelical churches the search for the unusual in religious experience predominates among at least ten percent of the religious community in America. Some have chosen retreat to the mystical in a search for the warm feelings about God and man which they deem lacking in established churches.

This constant search for religious expression outside established ways of knowing and feeling has helped to form a counter-culture identifiable by a new mind-set. When a young person says, "Do your own thing," or "It's not my bag," he is reflecting a new view of his world of experience. Zen Buddhism has made tremendous inroads into the youth of evangelical Christianity because it purports to offer direct contact with life and reality.

This withdrawal into the mystical is part of the search for the unusual because many have given up on established ways of knowing and feeling, including evangelical Christianity.

What the Cults Can Teach Evangelical Christianity

In each of the chapters which follow in this book, a section is included, usually entitled, "What They Can Teach Us." This is based on the fact that, once careful analysis replaces over-zealous negativism regarding these groups, it will become apparent that each brings several good points to the field of religious experience. This section is designed to spotlight what these groups as a whole can contribute to evangelical progress. These good points should be copied by evangelical Christians. An open view toward these alternative groups will replace the oversimplistic charts and swapping of proof-texts which has characterized most approaches by evangelical scholars toward these groups.

One evident manifestation of the alternative groups is their awareness and concentration on the importance of good public image. Mormons are known as good, moral people who care for their own. They are known as being patriotic citizens interested in public service. Through the Mormon Tabernacle Choir, they reach millions who know good music if not how to spot doctrinal deviation. More than a million visitors a year tour Temple Square in Salt Lake City. Mormons are known as being highly mission-minded and evangelistic, largely because of their two-year youth missions program. The Latter-Day Saints know growth comes partially through the maintenance of a good public image.

Christian Scientists are known as persons who care about healing in a despairing society. Through the award-winning newspaper, *The Christian Science Monitor,* they keep their positive personal and social viewpoints before the literate peoples of the world. Readily available are airport and main-street reading rooms with a friendly person nearby ready for conversation about spiritual matters.

British-Israelites, through such spokesmen as Garner Ted Armstrong and *The Plain Truth* magazine, knew the value of frequent and wise use of the mass media to disperse their message.

The Black Muslims recognize the importance of personal pietistic behavior. Refraining from the use of drugs including alcohol and tobacco is a mark of the Muslims. They also know the importance of the black male being the head of his house. Their image in the black community is one of pride in themselves because of their personal behavior.

Unitarian-Universalists are known as persons intellectually alert and socially active. They are part of the pattern within alternatives to discipleship to maintain a wholesome public image by keeping their interests in the public eye. Evangelical Christians have largely failed to concentrate enough of their efforts in this field. Much can be learned by careful observation of what the alternative groups are doing.

The groups discussed here have a second point to make to evangelical Christians. The role of evangelicals as evangelists has been usurped by others in the last two generations. The Latter-Day Saints have at least twenty thousand missionaries in the world. Jehovah's Witnesses make more than two hundred million visits in the United States annually. Garner Ted Armstrong is one of the most-heard voices in American radio. Black Muslims frequently pass out tracts on the front steps of black Protestant churches. Hare Krishna chanters do street preaching complete with free tracts and books. As Southern Baptists and other evangelical Christians become more respectable as established denominations, hopefully one-to-one witnessing will not be abandoned. Alternative groups have maintained personal contact as a part of established patterns of steady growth. Evangelical Christians should take note.

At least one other lesson can be learned from the alternative groups. Out of necessity, evangelical Christians will have to decide what is worth preserving in their strong tradition. A conservative view of the importance of the Bible as unique written revelation for every generation is part of evangelical strength. One who believes in the inerrancy of Scripture is forced today to be able to defend this view in the presence of those who advocate supplements to the Bible as being equal with it. Further, the finality of Christ among all religious prophets will have to be articulated constantly. Evangelical strength has always been partially based on proclamation. In the face of popular alternatives, a certain and relevant sound must continue to come from evangelical pulpits. In summary, the strong points of evangelicalism must be reinforced while learning from others who do have their own strong points.

On to More Study . . .

Christian discipleship is constantly threatened by well-meaning advocates of alternate gospels. This is no new phenomenon to this generation of the mid-1970's. It is as old as the assertion of God as a zealous God amid the other claimants to human allegiance.

The uniqueness of this generation, particularly in the United States, is based on the vast number of claimants to the truth and their freedom and ability to make their claims known through personal contact and the mass media.

Study and understanding are part of this generation's responsibility so as to be informed about the visitor who comes with *The Watch Tower* magazine or through "The World Tomorrow" radio program. There is no way to silence these alternate claims to discipleship, but one step in countering those claims is a better understanding of them *and* the teachings of the New Testament. So, on to more study . . .

Chapter 1

SAINTS AT HOME:
THE MORMONS

Dialogue: A Journal of Mormon Thought is an independent national quarterly established to examine the relevance of religion to secular life. The Summer, 1970, issue is typical in that it gives Mormon thinkers a place to air their doubts and affirm their faith simultaneously. One writer asks some significant questions:

> We Mormons have very definite concepts of the God we believe in, probably more definite than those of any other Christian group. Yet these distinctly anthropomorphic concepts of God raise significant questions. In what sense, for example, can God be omnipotent, omniscient, omnipresent, and all-good and at the same time be an individual with definite "body, parts, and passions"? Or how can He have these absolute attributes and still Himself be eternally progressing?[1]

More and more Mormons are beginning to think and question their faith. Formerly, many Mormons tended to think of their doctrine as constant and unchanging, influenced little by social surrounding. Observers of Mormonism from the outside returned the favor, thinking of the Latter-Day Saints as a stable, if not stagnant, group of believers in set dogma.

However, from the first revelations to Joseph Smith, Mormon thought has gathered from and reflected the ideas floating around it. Today is no exception. O. Kendall White observes a shift in social emphasis with sadness:

Contemporary Mormonism exhibits an apparent lack of concern for many of the world's most pressing problems. . . . In its literature, little concern with problems of war and peace, racial discrimination, poverty or population expansion is evident. Yet, few things characterized early Mormonism more than its concern for social justice and interest in creating the perfect society here on earth.[2]

Shifts in thought and action are part of modern Mormonism. All religious experience, especially in the United States, is subject to change. Unfortunately, most observers of other groups tend to want them to "stand still" while they observe. Most textbooks on the cults treat Mormonism as though it has been one frozen shape from the start. This is not the case, as a brief look at Mormon history reveals.

Joseph Smith and Followers

The movement called Mormonism owes its beginning to one boy turned man named Joseph Smith, Jr. He was born in Vermont in 1805 and was taken by his family to Palmyra, in western New York eleven years later. The area was a center of revivalistic fervor when Joseph arrived. Since evangelists came from various denominations, the identity of the true church was a popular topic of conversation.

Joseph had a vision in which a messenger told him that, despite his recent conversion, he was to join no church since they were all false. Three years later an angel named Moroni appeared to Joseph and told him where he would find some golden plates and their translating devices, the Urim and Thummim. Joseph later said he was forbidden by the angel to uncover the plates until some four years later in September, 1827.

In 1828, Joseph and a fairly wealthy farmer named Martin Harris started trying to translate the plates. They worked hard for two months. Mr. Harris showed more than a hundred pages of transcription to his wife who destroyed or hid the work. Mr. Smith responded by saying that he was warned in a vision not to give the same translation again verbatim. A new translation came out in the form of a book in 1830.

On April 6, 1830, only two weeks after the publication of the *Book of Mormon,* the "Church of Jesus Christ" was started with six members in Fayette, New York. In 1837, the name was changed to the Church of Jesus Christ of Latter-Day Saints. In 1831, Joseph led sixty followers to Kirtland, Ohio, where the first Mormon temple was built. There the movement picked up a new convert named Brigham Young.

In 1837, because of a severe banking failure, Joseph led his group of followers to Far West, Missouri, where over a thousand Mormons had already settled. Early in 1839, they were again forced to flee, this time to Nauvoo, Illinois. Within two years, Nauvoo was the largest city in Illinois with its own independent army. In 1844, a group of Saints became upset with their leader and accused Mr. Smith of polygamy. The charges were printed in a newspaper. Joseph was accused of destroying the newspaper office and was imprisoned in Carthage, Illinois, along with his brother, Hyrum. On June 27, 1844, the two were "martyred" while defending themselves from an irate mob which stormed the jail.

Naturally, a controversy arose over Joseph Smith's successor. His widow led a movement to place the leadership mantle on Joseph Smith III, their teen-age son. This group started meeting as the "New Organization of the Church" and is now known as the Reorganized Church of Jesus Christ of Latter-Day Saints and has its headquarters in Independence, Missouri. There are in 1972 more than a quarter of a million members.

Brigham Young was elected by the largest group in Nauvoo and in 1846 he and others set out for Utah. By 1867 the Salt Lake City Tabernacle was completed. Brigham Young died a decade later with more than one hundred fifty thousand followers to his credit.

Wilford Woodruff was one of the most famous presidents of the Church because he revoked the law of polygamy in 1890. David Mackay served from 1951 to 1970. He was succeeded by Joseph Fielding Smith, the current president, who is ninety-three years old.

Visible evidence of the spread of the Latter-Day Saints across America is the $14-million temple in the Washington, D.C., area due to be completed late in 1974. This will be the largest Mormon temple in the world. It is symbolic of the rapid growth of Mormonism in the last generation. In June, 1971, the Church of Jesus Christ of Latter-Day Saints passed the three million membership mark in the world. Current membership is more than 3,050,000 and is growing at an annual rate of more than 25,000.

Authority in Question

One dictionary defines authority as, "one that is claimed, or appealed to, in support of opinions, actions, measures, and so on . . . a book containing such a statement of opinion, or the author of the book."

A basic question when comparing religious groups is that of authority, i.e., where does one go to discern what he is to do or believe? For evangelical Christians, it has frequently been stated that the sole written authority is the Bible. Mormons contend that the Bible is a reliable authority on religious matters only when it is translated correctly. Even then, the Bible is supplemented for the Mormon by revelations to latter-day prophets.

Most Christians assert that God reveals himself to every generation through his distinctive written source—the Bible. The difference with Mormons comes in the question of whether another written revelation is needed. The Bible's worth is proven to every new generation in each epoch.

For the Latter-Day Saints, the *Book of Mormon* is the outstanding extrabiblical written source. However, it is an obvious example of a "modern" revelation which becomes obsolete rapidly. For the pioneer farmer of western New York in the 1820's, a question frequently discussed was the origin of the nearby Indian mounds and the men who built them. The *Book of Mormon* was added to an already impressive bibliography which sought to answer a contemporary question on the American frontier a century and a half ago, but a question not so crucial in the last fourth of the twentieth century.

Another revelation designed to guide modern saints is Joseph Smith's pronouncements on the place of the black American in society. In 1832, Joseph translated some Egyptian papyri which he recorded in the *Book of Abraham* 1:21–26. The translation is as follows:

Now this king of Egypt was a descendant from the loins of Ham and was a partaker of the blood of the Cannanites by birth. . . . Pharoah, being a righteous man, established his kingdom and judged his people wisely and justly all his days. . . . Noah, his father, blessed him with the blessings of wisdom, but cursed him as pertaining to the Priesthood.

The prophet Joseph Smith believed that *the Egyptians of ancient days were Negroid* and therefore black persons could not hold the priesthood. This "modern" revelation was possibly the result of the controversy over slavery going on in Missouri in the 1830's. Smith later spoke a revelation which still keeps black persons from marrying in a Mormon temple, holding the priesthood or entering into the celestial kingdom.

This latter-day revelation conflicts with Jesus' treatment of the Samaritan of his day or Saint Paul's statement that in the Savior there are no distinctions of culture, economics, or race (see Gal. 3:27–29), or even with humanitarian re-

spect for every person as having equal worth. A recent reve-
lation should be consistent with those which came before.
Evangelical Christians maintain that the authority of Christ
should be weighed when written revelation is interpreted.
This helps to guard from the mistake of interpreting the
Bible in any fashion that would not glorify Christ.

The Latter-Day Saints *rely* heavily for their doctrine on
the *Book of Mormon*. They claim that the work is a collection
of books originally written between the years 600 B.C. and
400 B.C. It allegedly deals with the history of the relation
between God and his chosen people on the Western
Hemisphere.

According to this book, a colony of Jews composed mainly
of people from the tribes of Ephraim and Manasseh, departed
from Jerusalem in the year 600 B.C. under the leadership of
a prophet named Lehi. Soon after their arrival in South
America, two of Lehi's sons—Nephi and Laman—fought and
the people chose sides. God was for Nephi, and he cursed the
Lamanites with a black skin. They became the forerunners
of the American Indians. The Nephites migrated northward
to Central America and were there when Christ visited them
right after his crucifixion.

The two factions began to fight again in the third century
and by A.D. 384 the Nephites were almost destroyed. This time
the Nephites were led by a priest named Mormon who, just
before the final battle, wrote a history of his people on some
golden plates and gave it to his son, Moroni. Moroni hid the
plates in what is now western New York and almost fifteen
centuries later appeared to young Joseph Smith to tell him of
the plates.

The *Book of Mormon* is made up of fourteen books and an
editorial note. The style is similar to that of the King James
Version of the Bible. The book is about six hundred pages
long. Some passages are direct quotes from the King James

Version, including "The Book of Mosiah" from Isaiah 53 and III Nephi 13:1–18 which is identical to Matthew 6:1–23.

The names used are closely related to those of biblical characters. They may be exactly alike such as Laban and Lemuel or close imitations such as Laman and Nephi. The finding of a promised land recalls Moses; the daughter of Jared dances before a king; and Alma's conversion is similar to Paul's. A central theme of the book is similar to a pattern presented in the "Chronicler" of the Old Testament: "Thus do we see how quick the children of men do forget the Lord their God, yea, how quick to do iniquity, and to be led away by the evil one" (Alma 46:8).

Non-Mormon students of American intellectual history have pointed frequently to the fact that the *Book of Mormon* is far from original in thought and reflects currents of thought common to the intellectual background of its day. Joseph Smith may have borrowed heavily from a writing by the Reverend Ethan Smith, a Vermont pastor. In 1823 he wrote *View of the Hebrews* and stated: "The red men had not long since a book which they had for a long time preserved. But having lost the knowledge of reading it, they concluded it would be of no further use to them; and they buried it with an Indian chief."[3]

Major parallels between the two works include: frequent references to the destruction of Jerusalem; inspired prophets among the ancient Americans; long quotes from Isaiah; pictures of the ancient Indians as a highly civilized people; and translation of ancient documents by use of the Urim and Thummim.[4]

The Latter-Day Saints include other works in their list of sacred literature. *The Pearl of Great Price* contains "The Book of Moses" of 1830 and "The Book of Abraham." The "Pearl" concludes with a portion of Matthew 24 and Mormonism's "Articles of Faith."

The book of *Doctrine and Covenants* was first published in Kirtland, Ohio, in 1835 and contains subsequent revelations, including the declaration prohibiting polygamy issued in 1890 by President Wilford Woodruff. Especially relevant to modern Mormons are the revelations about baptism for the dead and celestial marriage.

Mormons frequently refer to the "Word of Wisdom," which is Section 89 of *Doctrine and Covenants*. In a revelation received by Joseph Smith in 1833, he proclaimed:

Tobacco is not for the body, neither for the belly, and is not good for man. . . . Hot drinks are not for the body or belly. . . . And all saints who remember to keep and do these sayings, walking in obedience to the commandments, shall receive health in their navel and marrow to their bones; and shall find wisdom and great treasures of knowledge, even hidden treasures.[5]

This revelation forms the thought structure for the fact that devout Mormons do not drink hot tea or coffee.

The question of authority remains, "Does the Bible require further written authority for clarification and supplementation of its concepts?" For the modern Mormon the answer is in the affirmative. A popular Mormon study book contains this statement: "If we had no Bible, we would still have all the needed direction and information through the revelations of the Lord to his servants the prophets in these latter-days."[6]

Often the Bible is used to validate later revelations. Le Grand Richards supplies one reference to the Bible's meaning, amplified by the *Doctrine and Covenants:*

When one compares this complete explanation of the calling and duties and organization of the seventy with the meager account given in the Bible, he is convinced of the need for instruction and revelation from the Lord in these matters, since the Bible fails to give a sufficient account of the duties and calling of the seventy. Again we obtain this information and instruction by revelation from heaven, and we use the Bible to prove its truth.[7]

In effect, the Bible becomes a secondary source for determining the thought and practice of the Christian faith. The Mormon stance is clear, i.e., the Bible is to be used when in agreement with latter-day revelations. Many Christians find it difficult to believe that God would change his stance. Surely there must be a divine certainty about divine matters.

The key issue remains: Does the Holy Spirit speak to the believer adequately in the Bible and in Christ? For the Mormon, his (the Holy Spirit) work needs to be supplemented by further words which give added meaning to an inadequate Bible. Evangelical Christians have found that God reveals himself most clearly in Christ as seen through the Bible. Subsequent revelations have tended to detract from Christian discipleship.

Clarifications of the Bible's message by latter-day written sources fails three basic tests of divine revelation: an inherent self-consistency; a consistency with previous sacred revelations in a devotion and discipleship to the person of Christ.

Saintly Doctrines

A brief look at Latter-Day Saint doctrine reveals immediately that there is wide divergence from mainstream Christian thought. This is little known to most Christian laymen because terms are not defined sufficiently. Mormons use the same words as evangelical Christians, but with far different meaning.

God is portrayed as a superhuman with physical appearance. Joseph Smith had a revelation which said, "God himself was once a man as we are now and is an exalted man, and sits enthroned in yonder heavens."[8]

Jesus Christ in Mormon theology was a spirit-child of God as are all human beings and was born as the son of Adam-God and Mary. God is the father of the spiritual bodies of all mankind; Jesus is a brother of man. Jesus was supposed to have been a polygamist, having married two Marys and Martha at Cana.

Man is supposed to be an eternal being whose basic purpose is to become a god. He is preexistent to his earthly form. As Joseph Smith phrased it, man's eternal life consists of learning how to be a god, "By going from one small degree to another . . . until you . . . are able to dwell in everlasting burnings, and to sit in glory, as to those who sit enthroned in everlasting power."[9]

Latter-Day Saints speak out against what they call the false doctrine of one heaven and one hell. Instead, they teach three levels of salvation: celestial, terrestrial, and telestial. Mormons to be in the *celestial* realm are presently in an intermediate state called Paradise and will eventually be gods. The only persons eligible for this highest realm are those sealed in celestial marriage in the temple. The *terrestrial* level will be populated with Christians and members of other religions who did not accept the Mormon message. The *telestial* is reserved for those currently in hell who rejected the gospel and await the final resurrection.

Mormons invest much time and energy in their practice of baptism for the dead. The ceremony has been performed for more than thirty million persons, at a current annual rate of more than three million. The Genealogical Society employs more than five hundred people. This effort is expended because the Saints believe that the soul for which the baptism ceremonies is performed will approve of them and be saved.

According to Mormon doctrine, salvation is achieved by good works and is justly rewarded. Man achieves spiritual growth through obedience to God's laws. The "Articles of Faith" of the Church of Jesus Christ of Latter-Day Saints explains their official stance on the matter of salvation:

3. We believe that through the atonement of Christ all mankind will be saved, by obedience to the laws and ordinances of the gospel.
4. We believe that these ordinances are: 1st, Faith in the Lord Jesus Christ; 2nd, Repentance; 3rd, Baptism by immersion for the remission of sins; 4th, Laying on of hands for the gift of the Holy Spirit; 5th, the Lord's Supper.

Mormons believe that God intervened in American history to establish the one true Church. They classify Christian churches in three categories: Catholics who believe that the true church has had an uninterrupted existence since Jesus Christ; Protestants who contend that the true church fell into apostasy and must be restored according to the Bible, but who cannot interpret without further written revelation; and a restoration movement which has the only true latter-day revelation.

The Saints have combined restorationist views toward revelation with the American dream. They believe that the true Zion will be built on the American continent.

The doctrinal system which the "true" church and its prophets produced was a mixture of themes based on Campbellite thought, frontier dreams, pragmatic schemes for self-improvement, and biblical truth. It is a system with shifting emphases, but one which can remain patriotic and religious, if not thoroughly Christian.

Mormon Morality

By many popular standards, Mormons are good moral people. They are said to be industrious, resourceful, patriotic, and temperate. They are forbidden to smoke, drink alcohol, or even indulge in hot coffee or tea. They must also give 10 percent of their gross income to the Church.

The Latter-Day Saints are known as a people who care

for their own members. Since 1936 they have supported a church welfare program which distributes life's necessities to the poor, finds jobs for their unemployed, and improves living conditions among their low-income families. The bishops have a fund for emergency money needs. No one receiving public welfare funds can receive aid from the Mormon Church.

A negative aspect of the Mormon ethical system is the denying of the right of priesthood to Negroes. The official stance is as follows: "Negroes and other people with Negroid blood can become members of the church. . . . but they cannot be ordained to the priesthood, nor are they eligible for marriage in an LDS temple."[10]

The first Federal bill to prohibit polygamous marriages was introduced into the United States Congress in 1860. The "Edmunds Law" of 1881 imposed heavy fines and imprisonments on polygamists as well as denied them the right to vote. All this led to a manifesto from Mormon President Woodruff in September, 1890, which stated the intention of the Utah group to submit to the law regarding plural marriage.

Seven of the ten Latter-Day Saints' presidents have been polygamists. At no time, however, has more than 15 percent of the total Mormon membership participated in polygamy. A current estimate is that about twenty-thousand Mormons still practice plural marriage in spite of official warnings.

Joseph Smith relied heavily on the Old Testament in forming his system of ethical teachings. He stressed a strong communal relationship with ties of fellowship and practical guidelines to care for the needy similar to the Hebrew commonwealth. Unfortunately, the same negative attitude toward the outsider prevalent in the Old Testament along with the supposed curse on certain descendants of Noah prevails in the Mormon establishment. The same "second-class" position of women evident in Jewish life, B.C., can be seen today in the Mormon concept of marriage, both temporal and celestial. The statement that Mormons are good people must be understood in light of the fact that they have failed to emphasize sufficiently the New Testament ethic, especially the life and teachings of Jesus in relation to women and "strangers."

What Mormons Can Teach Evangelical Christians

The Latter-Day Saints have shown a constant capacity for growth in the United States. There are many reasons for this growth despite their largely unbiblical doctrine. One primary factor is the fact that many Mormons are "true believers," i.e., they are willing to stand firmly on their beliefs. Mormon Church leaders have rejected several approaches by this author to set up a Mormon-Baptist dialogue gathering on a nationwide basis. Their doctrine is inherently reasonable when kept in a closed system with its own presuppositions such as man's innate capacity for godhood. Often these ideas are successfully mingled with a careful emphasis on the parallels between Mormonism and traditional Christianity to proselyte those who are labeled Christian. Mormon certainty is largely based on careful education and training within their wards. Evangelicals would do well to emulate the Mormon stress on training in correct doctrine.

Mormons utilize a common American idea on religious experience which suggests that if one, or a group of people, lives morally then his doctrines do not really matter. The Mormon welfare system and refraining from unhealthy physical habits do commend the Saints to outside observers who do not closely examine Mormon doctrine. Christian ministry to those in distress is a part of the Christian faith which should be taken seriously by those who hope to impress upon the Mormon the importance of correct belief concerning the eternal nature of God the Father and Christ. A renewed emphasis on the unique value of man is in order for the entire Christian camp.

The Mormon missionary program, which sends young persons out to invest two years of their lives, has been a very effective method of Mormon proselyting. Other religious groups, such as Southern Baptists, have similar two-year programs which stress a deeper involvement with human problems than were house-to-house discussions. The Special Missions Ministries Department of the Home Mission Board, SBC, has launched an experimental one-year program for college-age youth called "Youth on Mission." Early reports indicate meaningful ministry coming from the program. The youth's period of service is financed by Baptist parents, somewhat similar to the Mormon plan. The Latter-Day Saints have a missionary program that has been largely successful in terms of numbers. With some adaptation, it should be emulated by evangelical groups.

The Mormon system of theological institutes and seminaries also deserves closer examination and possible emulation. Institutes of religion are maintained near colleges in five western states, involving over six thousand students. They are located adjacent to high schools and their courses are often accredited through the public school system. This educational system helps to conserve the young students for the Mormon faith.

The Mormon Tabernacle Choir is symbolic of the effort by the Latter-Day Saints to create and maintain a wholesome public image. Each year more than a million visitors see the Mormon Temple Square in Salt Lake City. The missionary program helps to create for the Saints an image of concern for others. Ask most non-Mormons about the Latter-Day Saints, and they will reply that the Mormons are a strongly patriotic people who care for their own. Evangelical Christians can learn from the Mormons the value of molding a wholesome public image, particularly through the press. In this mass media age, image is crucial in attracting converts.

How to Witness

Unfortunately, the initiative of door-to-door witnessing has been with the Mormons. The initiative should be in the hands of born-again Christians. Until this happens, the following steps are recommended for evangelical Christians when approached by a pair of Mormon missionaries:

1. Be polite.
2. Be certain that terms are well-defined by the Mormons.
3. Settle the place of the *Book of Mormon* very early in the conversation.
4. Focus the conversation on present joy in certain knowledge of eternal salvation.
5. Visit the Mormon missionaries the same day.

Open discussion of Mormon history is helpful in the witnessing process as friendship grows and communication stays open. Common reading and discussion of such works as the chapter on Mormonism in *Freedom's Ferment*[11] can be helpful in making the Latter-Day Saint aware of his own shaky heritage.

Exchange of proof-texts out of context is seldom helpful in witnessing to Mormons. However, there will be times in common Bible study with the Mormon that these sections will be helpful:

1. Salvation—1 John 5:9–13; James 1:5–7; Matthew 22: 37–38.
2. Sin—John 8:31–36.
3. Holy Spirit—John 15.

4. Jesus Christ—1 Thessalonians 4:13–18; John 17:3–5; Colossians 1:16–17.
5. God, the Father—John 4:24.

These verses should be readily available as the conversation progresses toward the goal of personal salvation.

Chapter II

JEHOVAH'S WITNESSES:
JESUS IS SECOND BEST

In the calendar year 1971, Jehovah's Witnesses around the world spent more than three hundred million hours talking to others about spiritual matters. They made more than 140 million return visits at the request of those visited because of their eagerness to share their understanding of Jehovah. More than two million hours were spent in home Bible studies.

More than six hundred new Witnesses were baptized recently in Atlanta, Georgia. They were told at their baptism: "You have come to a busy organization. . . . Work hard in your ministry because we are living in a time of great urgency. The time remaining is short. . . . We work hard because we want to make up for the past neglect of God's will."

Those in the crowd were asked two questions to which they replied in the affirmative. They were: (1) Have you recognized yourself before Jehovah as a sinner who needs salvation, and have you acknowledged to him that this salvation proceeds from him, the Father, through his Son, Jesus Christ? (2) Have you dedicated yourself unreservedly to God to do his will henceforth as he reveals it to you through Jesus Christ and through the Bible under the enlightening power of the holy spirit?

The new Witnesses were then welcomed as "happy, hardworking servants" with a clear understanding of Jehovah's will and purpose.[1] These new Jehovah's Witnesses were being welcomed to a life characterized by zeal and urgency as part of an army to announce the eminent end of the world.

Brief History

Though most of the Jehovah's Witnesses living today insist that their beginning was in the mind and heart of God, the outside observer might well contend that the movement began in the person of Charles Taze Russell. He was born in 1852 in Pittsburgh. His parents were Presbyterians but he joined the Congregationalists because they were more liberal. By age of seventeen, he gave up on his church, primarily because of their teachings of a literal hell. In 1870 he started visiting Seventh-Day Adventist meetings. There he met five others who were interested in a small group Bible study. They soon reached the conclusion that Christ's second coming was to be invisible, or of the spirit. This conclusion was embodied in Russell's first writing attempt, a pamphlet entitled, "The Object and Manner of Our Lord's Return." On July 1, 1879, Russell published a new magazine entitled *Zion's Watch Tower*. As *The Watchtower* it has never ceased publication.

At this stage Mr. Russell toured the United States, trying to set up congregations wherever he could. In 1881 his organization was formed. World missions was part of Russell's vision from the beginning. In 1900 a branch office was opened in London.

Mr. Russell and his followers began to announce that the end of the world was to come in 1914. When this failed to happen, the Society's literature was not so popular. Distribution went from more than seventy-one million in 1914 to just over thirty million in 1916. Russell died a disappointed man in 1916 while on a tour in west Texas. His life was characterized by the same urgency and disappointment as hundreds of others who try to predict the exact date of the world's end.

The leadership of the movement passed to "Judge" Rutherford (1869–1942), who gave the Society the optimistic, fresh leadership it needed through a new beginning and an economic depression. Rutherford came up with the slogan, "Millions Now Living Will Never Die." He wrote 22 full-length books, dozens of pamphlets, and supervised the circulation of almost one-half billion pieces of literature. In 1931 the name of the group was changed to "Jehovah's Witnesses." Rutherford gave form to much of the present organizational structure. He also introduced the popular magazine entitled, *Awake*. The "Judge" died in 1942, having already named his successor.

Nathan Knorr (1905–   ) has served as president of the organization since 1942. He had served as general manager of the publishing office and plant since 1932. Efficiency has characterized his reign as leader of the Witnesses. Knorr has popularized the idea among the Witnesses that "light has no fellowship with darkness." The Witnesses are to steer clear of this evil world and all its political and religious systems. The future of the Jehovah's Witnesses is difficult to predict, but steady growth is probable because of the Witnesses' zeal.

Basic Beliefs

Many persons presently evangelical Christians would not be attracted to Jehovah's Witness teaching if they were aware of the way the Witnesses use the Bible to prove their points. This author took an impromptu survey of one hundred Witness adults at an International Peace Assembly in 1969. Two questions were asked, "Did you become a Jehovah's Witness as an adult?" and, "If so, what group did you formerly belong to?" Sixty-one answered in the affirmative to the first question and forty-one said they were formerly Baptists. This is indicative of the Witness appeal to those with a general respect for Scripture, but with little knowledge of biblical interpretation.

The following points will soon become evident in conversation with Jehovah's Witnesses:

1. They make much use of the apocalyptic literature of the Bible (Daniel and the Revelation) in their formulation of doctrine.
2. Prophecy is thought to be primarily prediction of the future rather than the biblical idea of being God's spokesman in the present tense.
3. All biblical texts are treated as being on the same level of value. The context is usually considered irrelevant.
4. Proof texts are used to support Witness beliefs, even if these texts do not naturally fit together and have to be forcibly thrown together to strengthen a point.
5. The Bible is seen to be highly literal, with little attention given to different forms, such as poetry.

Most any point of doctrine can be "proven" if the Bible is treated in this manner. That is why it is necessary often to discuss the nature of the Bible with a Jehovah's Witness before intelligent talk about beliefs can occur.

Jehovah's Witnesses generally agree with the following statements:

1. *Who Is God?*
   The Almighty God is Jehovah. . . . By his name Jehovah he is distinguished from all the pagan gods of heathendom.
2. *Who Is Jesus Christ?*
   Jesus Christ, a created individual, is the second greatest personage in the universe. Jesus was formed countless millenniums ago as the first and only direct creation by His Father, Jehovah. . . . Because of his proved, faultless integrity, Jesus was appointed by Jehovah as his cindicator and Chief Agent of Life toward mankind. . . .
3. *What Is the True Church?*
   . . . The church consists of 144,000 associates with Christ,

resurrected to the heavens as kings and priests with him. . . .
4. *What Is the Seriousness of Our Day?*
   We are living in the time of the consummation of the present system of things. . . . The preaching of this good news of God's established kingdom world-wide is the foremost evidence of all. . . .
5. *How Will This Present World End?*
   This world will end at the "war of the great day of God the Almighty" called in the Scriptures, "Armageddon." At this time, Jehovah's executive officer, Christ Jesus, will lead invisible forces of righteousness to destroy Satan and his demonic and human organization. . . .
6. *Who Can Survive the World's End?*
   Those who exercise faith in Jehovah God and publicly proclaim the truth, thus receiving God's favor, can survive Armageddon and find themselves directly on the road to life on earth in the new system. . . .[2]

Witness doctrine has been under severe attack by many in other groups called Christian for almost a century now. Much of the criticism is deserved, when viewed from an evangelical Christian base.

Jehovah's Witnesses claim that the doctrine of the Trinity originated with Satan. The Holy Spirit is not a divine Person at all but "the invisible, active force of Almighty God which moves his servants to do his will."[3] In this regard, the Witnesses can be said to be strict Unitarians. They see Jehovah existing as a solitary person.

The Witnesses' treatment of Jesus Christ is a serious problem to evangelical Christians. He is only second best in their system of thought; he is seen only as Jehovah's chief assistant. He is superior to all other creatures but never equal to the Father. Before Jesus came to earth, he was an angel known as Michael. Therefore, when Jesus was born of Mary, it was not the incarnation of God, but only the birth of a created person.

This low view of Jesus carries over into the Witness view of the resurrection. Jehovah supposedly raised Christ from the dead, "not as a human Son but as a mighty immortal spirit."[4]

Jehovah's Witnesses give complete allegiance to Jehovah rather than to the state. They refuse to bear arms and in time of war attempt to remain neutral. They refuse to salute the flag of any nation because all kingdoms of this world are evil. To salute the flag would be image worship. The Witnesses claim exemption from military service for all of their members because all of them are viewed as full-time ministers. They refuse to vote, to hold public office, and to take part in most civic affairs. During World War II more than seven thousand Witnesses were placed in Federal prisons rather than renounce their beliefs. They do make the concession of paying taxes and obeying those laws which they consider not to be in opposition to the will of Jehovah. Very seldom does the child of a Witness family go on to attend college. The public education system is viewed as evil and the sooner it can be abandoned, the better.

The Witnesses hold that death is really unconsciousness or extinction. Death is "loss of life; termination of existence,"[5] and can be proven by such texts as Psalm 13:3 and Daniel 12:2. The Witnesses teach that the doctrine of a burning hell cannot be true for four reasons: it is wholly unscriptural (Note: Some Bible scholars may wonder about this); it is unreasonable, it is contrary to God's love; and it is repugnant to justice.[6]

A Critical Analysis

The largest issue in any religious discussion is that of authority, i.e., "What can be used to find what one is to believe?" and "How do we apply that source of authority?"

The Jehovah's Witnesses are not content simply to use the proof-text method of biblical interpretation; they also have translated the Scriptures for their own group. It is entitled,

The New World Translation of the Holy Scriptures. The New
Testament version alone sold almost a half-million copies in
its first year, 1950–1951.

The Witness gets no encouragement to interpret the Bible
for himself. The Watch Tower Society does this for him, passing on the "truth" without question. An example of this appears in the Bible-study handbook, *Let God Be True,* in
which the writer quotes their own translation to prove the
point that Christ was not always equal to God. *The New
World Translation* renders John 1:1–2: "And the Word was
a god."[7] It is clear that, to the true believer among Jehovah's
Witnesses, the Society and not the Bible, is the final authority.

If the evangelical Christian grants the person whom he
encounters in discussion of Christian beliefs the right to use
his own translation of the Bible and to employ the method of
running proof texts together without discrimination, and if he
grants the validity of the other person's own closed system
whereby his group tells him what the Bible means, then there
is little hope for common study of the written Word and for
sharing of belief. Until the question of authority is resolved,
there is little hope for a sharing witness. It is necessary to
settle the question of authority before fruitful discussion can
occur.

There are also vital differences between Jehovah's Witnesses and evangelical Christians regarding the living Word—
the risen Savior. Radical surrender to a Christ who has conquered death and a daily awareness of his presence cannot
be sacrificed by an evangelical Christian. As Paul phrased
it, "If there be no resurrection of the dead, then is Christ
not risen. And if Christ be not risen then is our preaching
vain, and your faith is also vain" (1 Cor. 15:13–14). Evangelical Christians affirm that the man Jesus was fully human
and fully divine.

Evangelical Christians can learn a lesson in reverse from

the Witnesses. The Witnesses largely have become other-worldly to the extent of neglecting their neighbors. The love by which Christians are to be known involves a wholesome attitude toward this world. Otherwise, Jesus would never have taken time in his short ministry to preach the greatest guide to human living of all time—the Sermon on the Mount. By considering the total biblical witness, the Christian should deem it his responsibility to keep a healthy tension between his salvation in this world and the eternal hope of the coming Lord. Paul expressed this tension in 2 Corinthians 5:8–9: "We are confident, I say, and willing rather to be absent from the body, and to be present with the Lord. Wherefore we labor, that, whether present or absent, we may be acccpted of him."

What They Can Teach Us

Jehovah's Witnesses are practitioners of the priesthood of the believers. While some Protestants are stressing doctrinally that same priesthood, the Witnesses are practicing it. Each Witness is expected to spend at least five hours a week knocking on doors. He is called a minister. His priesthood does not include the right to interpret for himself however.

The Witnesses place a strong emphasis on a tight family unit. They pray together, attend Bible studies together, and witness door-to-door together. When visiting large gatherings of Witnesses, one is impressed with the family units eating, sitting, walking, and listening together. Outside activities are chosen carefully. When possible, the whole family enjoys recreation together.

Jehovah's Witnesses win many converts among minority groups in America. At least half of the crowd of Witnesses at a large assembly in Atlanta was black. There is little or no evidence of racial discrimination among the Witnesses. The Witnesses continue to attract chiefly the outcasts of society.

These are the forgotten people of an affluent society who are distrustful of the world situation partly because they are being ignored by the larger denominations. These are the very ones in whom Jesus took such a vital interest during his earthly ministry.

Sixty-five percent of the Jehovah's Witnesses go out witnessing regularly every month. Posters, magazines, and advertisements can never replace the man so "sold" on his Savior that he wants his neighborhood to know him. Emulation of the strong points of the Witnesses is in order for evangelical Christians.

How to Witness to a Witness

Nothing is to be gained by arrogant condemnation of the group called Jehovah's Witnesses, especially in the matter of personal witnessing. If the individual Witness is to be reached with the gospel, a good beginning is to listen appreciatively to what he is saying. He has much to say that is, in a way, a condemnation of the Baptist neglect of certain biblical truths.

If the Witness does not listen the first time the gospel message is presented, show deep personal interest in him as a person. Merely to prove him wrong is to lose him, as far as any responsible witness is concerned. Most sociologists who study the Jehovah's Witnesses agree that they are not "at home" in this world for varied economic or cultural reasons. Concerned prayer, sharpened Bible tools used intelligently, and deep personal concern such as Jesus showed for the social outcasts of his day form the basic hope for evangelical Christians in presenting the risen Christ to a sincere Jehovah's Witness.

The following procedure is recommended for evangelical Christians when they are confronted at their front door by a Witness:

1. Greet the visitor courteously. Give your name and ask his name. Ask if he lives in the neighborhood. Invite him in for a few minutes.
2. Indicate an appreciation for his zeal in spreading his faith and his interest in matters of religion.
3. Allow him to go through his first ten-minute presentation of what the Witnesses are emphasizing that particular month.
4. Buy any literature he has. He has paid for it out of his own pocket.
5. Ask leading questions which allow the Witness to affirm his own faith. An example is, "What has being a Jehovah's Witness done for your family?"
6. Give positive testimony of faith in Christ, stressing peace and joy in the life of the Christian disciple.
7. Merely to win the first argument with the Jehovah's witness is often to lose him. Close off this first interview in about twenty minutes.
8. Plan quick follow-up action. The best procedure is to go to see the Witness the very same day. This will allow him to see that his zeal in witnessing has been matched. It is good at this point to give the Witness a copy of *Good News For Modern Man*. Introduction of a new translation will allow some new thoughts to flow through the continuing conversation.

As the friendship develops, some verses may be of help in the running discussion. They are:

1. The Deity of Christ—John 20:25–28.
2. Holy Spirit—John 16:7–14.
3. Resurrection—John 2:14–21.
4. Repentance—John 3.

Even better than studying isolated sections is a mutual study of one book in the Bible, such as Colossians. Be sure to use modern translations and to go verse-by-verse. Stress a common search for truth rather than a carefully-veiled fight to prove respective points.

Above all, pray for the grace to care enough to be patient and for the continuing leadership of the Holy Spirit.

Chapter III

ANGLO-ISRAELISM
AND THE ARMSTRONGS

From Herbert W. Armstrong's article in *Tomorrow's World* entitled, "Just What Do You Mean . . . Born Again?" comes these words:

> Being born again refers to the time—the future state—when we shall be spirit, no longer flesh and blood—born actually by the resurrection. . . .
> We are now begotten children of God. . . not yet spirit-composed divine beings—not yet inheritors—not yet having been "brought forth" into, or seen, or inherited the Kingdom of God—therefore, not yet born of God.[1]

This is but one among the dozens of articles and pamphlets available each month from Pasadena, California, the headquarters of the Worldwide Church of God. This movement is but one expounding the views of Anglo-Israelism. Coupled with basically legalistic doctrines regarding salvation, the Anglo-Israel movement offers an alternative to discipleship.

History of the Movement

In 1840, an Englishman named John Wilson wrote *Our Israelitish Heritage,* claiming to connect Great Britain with the lost tribe of Ephraim. About thirty years later another book appeared entitled *The Identification of the British Nation with the Lost Tribes of Israel* and written by Edward

Hines. The two books postulated similar theories, as indicated in the titles.

In 1879 the first Anglo-Israel association was founded in England. The next year a periodical was started in the United States under the title, *Heirs of the World*. By the turn of the century, as many as two million persons held to the Anglo-Israel views in the two nations.

In 1928, M. H. Gayer of London wrote one of the standard works of the movement, *The Heritage of the Anglo-Saxon Race*. The book included an elaborate chart "proving" that Great Britain and the United States are really the lost tribes of Ephraim and Manasseh.

Burhl B. Gilpin published a book in 1966 entitled *All Israel* which tries to demonstrate that the Bible is primarily a history of the Israelites. He also expounds the view that Jesus and Joseph of Arimathea visited the British Isles before Christ was thirty years of age. This theory is based on "a strong and persistent tradition in southwestern England that Christ visited the British Isles during that period."[2]

Another current example of Anglo-Israelism's life in the United States is the Anglo-Saxon Federation of America, publishers of *Destiny* magazine. The credendum or doctrinal statement on which the magazine is founded says: "The information published in *Destiny* provides the evidence showing that Israel left Palestine while the Jews remained. The movements of the Israel clans are traced out of the East, across Europe, to their new settlement in the Isles of Britain, and then on to America."[3]

The creed is complete with a warning to those who doubt its premises and conclusions:

When it is recognized universally that the Anglo-Saxon-Celtic peoples are modern Israel, opponents of this truth who have succeeded in leading many astray, and hindered to that extent the national repentance and return to God in wholehearted acknowledgment of his sovereignty and obedience to his laws, will discover that he will not hold them guiltless.[4]

By far the most active exponents of the Anglo-Israel theory today are the followers of Herbert W. Armstrong and his articulate son, Garner Ted Armstrong. Herbert W. Armstrong grew up in Iowa, drank heavily from the wells of Seventh-Day Adventism, and combined those views with Anglo-Israelism. He began his radio ministry in 1934. It has expanded now to include twenty-two million regular listeners around the world. More than one-hundred thirty stations carry the radio broadcast entitled, "The World Tomorrow" in the United States. That number is duplicated in the rest of the world. A conservative estimate of the Armstrongs' annual current budget is $7,000,000. Ambassador College, on three campuses, has more than fourteen hundred students. A beautiful four-color magazine, *The Plain Truth*, has two million monthly subscribers. *Tomorrow's World* is a popular magazine also distributed by the Worldwide Church of God. Garner Ted Armstrong does most of the radio and television speaking now and is one of the top ten in popularity in American radio.

The future of Anglo-Israelism depends heavily on Garner Ted Armstrong. With his father growing older and lesser groups within the Anglo-Israel movement growing weaker, the younger Armstrong already carries much of the load of expounding this theory. Its basic message has never been carried to such a broad audience, however, and Anglo-Israelism appears to be in very capable hands.

A crisis arose late in 1971 and got public attention in mid-1972 which produced a rift between the elder Armstrong and his son. Garner Ted Armstrong was replaced on radio broadcasts by older recorded tapes by the founder. At the time this book was written, the rift continued.

Beliefs

The fundamental statement which makes the Anglo-Israel faith different from other theories is that Britain is the lost tribe of Ephraim and the United States is really Manasseh. This conclusion is arrived at after an intricate outline of "facts" which leads the student from Eden to Pasadena. Anglo-Israelites base much of their findings on the theory that about five sixths of the Bible is written to and about Israel.

In his free book, *The United States and the British Commonwealth in Prophecy,* Herbert W. Armstrong traces the process of England and America being lost tribes and warns the reader that to ignore this "truth" is to doubt the infallibility of the Bible.

The principal beliefs expounded by Armstrong may be summarized:

1. The Jews are only one nation of which Abraham is the father.
2. Genesis 48 records the event in which Jacob adopted Joseph's two sons, Ephraim and Manasseh. So the name of Israel applies only to these two sons and their descendants.
3. The house of Israel is *not* Jewish. The Jews are of the house of Judah only.

Armstrong "proves" the fact that Britain is really Ephraim, "The Royal Family of the British Commonwealth possesses a chart showing its ancestry, every generation, back to Herremon and Tephi, to Zedekiah, on back to David, and through the scriptural genealogy clear to Adam."[5]

For the objective scholar, the fact that British royalty has a chart tracing them back to Adam through David is a bit unimpressive.

The free book closes with the conclusion of this research,

which is a bit exclusive in calling only the chosen people to repent:

> This terrifyingly severe punishment is, simply, the correction our peoples have made necessary to bring them to the ways of living which cause desired blessings, instead of terrible curses. . . . This book gives the warning from God and His Word! Will the U.S. and British nations heed?[6]

The chart which the British royalty holds and to which Armstrong refers is that contained in Gayer's *The Heritage of the Anglo-Saxon Race,* in which the author supplies "proof" of this historical movement of Ephraim to the British Isles.

> They seem to have first settled in Scandinavia, where they became known as Norsemen or Normans, from dwelling in the North. If this is true, the tribes of Joseph and Benjamin—separated for nearly eighteen centuries—met once more in Normandy, and though unconscious of each other's identity, entered together as one people into Britain.[7]

As in the case of Herbert W. Armstrong, Gayer strings together the proof of his findings through several sources: "The history of Israel runs through the Bible, up to the time of her captivity in Assyria. The Apocrypha then carries the story a step further. Here Bible history ends. Next, Bible prophecy steps in, and in veiled language tells us what is happening to the race."[8]

For Armstrong, the reason the Bible has been misunderstood so long is that the "vital key, needed to unlock prophetic doors to understanding, had become lost. That key is a definite knowledge of the true identity of the American and British peoples in Biblical prophecy."[9]

This is but an echo of what Gayer wrote forty years earlier, "Christian truth and Israel truth are so interwoven that neither is complete without the other."[10]

More truths are evident to those who believe in "Israel-truth." These truths go unseen by most Christians who do not have the "key" to Bible knowledge.

One truth has become a dominant theme in *The Plain Truth* magazine, the rebuilding of the Roman Empire. The issue for March, 1967 (p. 49), says: "The threat of Communism is not the only danger to America. Rising out of the ashes of World War II is a new menace to the free world, a seventh and last, resurrection of the ancient Roman Empire." A subsequent issue of *The Plain Truth* has on the cover a picture of British Prime Minister Wilson visiting Bonn, Germany. The lead article explains the significance of the visit:

Modern Germany is Assyria in Biblical prophecy . . . Your Bible describes exactly what is taking place in Bonn right now! . . . When Ephraim (identified in Bible prophecy as Britain) saw his sickness (his helpless economic plight) then went Ephraim to the Assyrian. (Hosea 5:3).[11]

A gentle reminder of this type of selective reasoning, which seeks to make the Bible relevant by going to great lengths to relate it to specific current events, is the fact that forty years previously the leader of the Anglo-Israel movement had some predictions about Germany based loosely on the Bible. According to Gayer, Gomer in Ezekiel 38:2 referred to Germany; and he wrote:

Russia and Germany have been in secret alliance since 1922. . . . Germany, through her military and technical instructors, is reconstructing Russia, and exploiting its enormous resources, in the hope that she and her ally will someday attain their dream of world dominance.[12]

A second truth revealed to adherents ,of the British-Israel theory is the nature of the world tomorrow. A basic premise of this theory is that the present civilization cannot be saved, especially by existing churches. The Armstrongs and their Worldwide Church of God condemn the churches frequently for "teaching the diametric opposite of Christ's teachings."[13] In the same spirit. the Armstrongs write in another of their booklets, "We are deceived into a counterfeit Christianity our lands are filled with false ministers . . ."[14] For the Armstrongs, the true answer is for more people to join the Worldwide Church of God. They predict that during the great tribulation, "hundreds of thousands will remember the true message from God that they heard going out freely to the world at this time, on 'The World Tomorrow' program."[15]

A third truth evident to the Anglo-Israelite is that of who will rule the Gentiles in the future new world. A booklet by Herbert W. Armstrong gives the answer: "There is a strong indication—not a define specific statement—but indication, according to principles and specific assignments that are revealed, that the prophet Daniel will be made king over them all, directly under Moses."[16]

Also, it seems evident to the Armstrongs that the resurrected Noah will head a vast project of the relocation of the races and nations.

Apart from its Anglo-Israelism, the Worldwide Church of God teaches other doctrines which run counter to evangelical Christianity. Most of these doctrines are related directly to Seventh-Day Adventism. They include the following:

1. Salvation is by faith in Jesus Christ by which one is enabled to keep the Law. Salvation will be given only to those who keep the Law. Herbert W. Armstrong concludes one of his booklets by describing the saved person:

> If you do turn to God by forsaking your way and this world's way through Jesus Christ as your personal Saviour—if you do then overcome—if you pray earnestly and continually . . . and endure in this wonderful new life, you shall be accounted worthy to escape all these terrifying things soon to befall the world.[17]

One issue of *The Plain Truth* makes the point clearer concerning salvation, "Assuredly this believing on Christ is necessary, yet other biblical passages make plain that this is not all that constitutes 'being saved.' "[18]

The definition of a Christian, for Armstrong is, "One who has, at the moment, God's Holy Spirit dwelling in him."[19]

It appears that the Christian must live in constant fear of losing the presence of the Holy Spirit at any given moment. If he should die at a time when the Holy Spirit is absent, he is doomed. This system gives the Christian no assurance of his salvation but develops instead a growing fear of losing God's spirit at any time. The Armstrongs seem to ignore 2 Timothy 1:7, "For God has not given us the spirit of fear, but of power, and of love, and of a sound mind."

2. The Armstrongs face one of the perpetual problems of the Adventist, that of periodically setting the date and manner of Christ's return. One of their basic assumptions is that the end of the world is coming in this generation, although the Armstrongs have backed away from 1975 as the specific date for the beginning of the end. In a booklet written in 1966, the Armstrongs say, "We can't set definite dates, remember! But this new World Tomorrow appears to be not too much farther off than 1966—or even 1987—it's coming in our time."[20] This is in direct contrast to earlier writings, which were much more definite about 1975.

3. The Worldwide Church of God teaches that the majority of those who die without belief in Christ will be resurrected and given opportunity to believe during the millenium.

4. For the Armstrongs, the seventh day of the week is the true sabbath of the New Testament church.

5. God is seen as the only true physician. Medicine supposedly has a pagan origin. Most sickness and disease today is the result of faulty diet. Herbert W. Armstrong labels all forms of healing outside of faith in God as idolatry.[21]

6. The Armstrongs believe that baptism is essential to salvation. Herbert W. Armstrong wrote:

Then once you have made up your mind to yield to God, and to become a member of His Church—not some denomination, WRITE TO US immediately, telling us that you want to be baptized this summer. Plans are already being laid for baptizing tours to cover the United States and other areas of the world.[22]

The Worldwide Church of God combines Anglo-Israelism with other doctrines deviant from evangelical Christianity. It poses a major threat to born-again believers in Christ.

A Critical Analysis

The Anglo-Israel movement is too narrow in its scope or plan for world redemption. The emphasis is almost solely on the need for repentance in Britain and America—the lost tribes of Ephraim and Manasseh—and has little concern for the more than two billion other people in the world. Instead, the emphasis is on "the race" and its purity, coupled with its obligation. Every evaluation of the present and future world situation is made in the light of western Europe alone.

Another possible weakness of Anglo-Israelism is its indiscriminate use of the Bible in an attempt to spell out in detail the world tomorrow. Proof texts are often grabbed at random out of context, with little regard for background. One prime example of such irresponsible use of Scripture is the Armstrongs' attempt to prove that Anglo-Saxons are Israelites:

To Abraham, God said, "In Isaac shall thy seed be called," and this name is repeated in Romans 9:7, Hebrews 11:18. In Amos 7:16 they are called the "house of Isaac."
They were descended from Isaac, and therefore are Isaac's sons. Drop the "I" from Isaac, vowels are not used in Hebrew spelling, and we have the modern name, Saac's sons, or, as we spelled it in shorter manner, Saxons.[23]

Evangelical Christians have a deep reverence for the Bible and for anyone who uses the Bible as a guide for faith and practice. However, proper attention must be given to context, occasion of writing and historical significance for its own day. To quote a verse out of context is to prove nothing.

Two other possible weaknesses of Anglo-Israelism, described in the previous section, are the attempt to set the specific date for the end of the world and the detailed spelling-out of its consequences to the point of stretching biblical meaning. For the devoted evangelical Christian, his trust is in his risen Lord, who will return in time, rather than faith in a well articulated scheme. These weaknesses have historically been a part of Adventist schemes to determine how and when Jesus will return.

A final weakness of the Worldwide Church of God is not necessarily related to Anglo-Israelism. The Armstrongs fail to maintain the biblical balance between law and gospel. The grace and forgiveness stressed in the New Testament is virtually overlooked by these radio prophets.

What They Can Teach Us

Evangelical Christians stand to learn a lot from the Armstrongs' questioning of the tenets of some forms of evolutionary reasoning concerning the origin of man. This problem should be approached intelligently by pastors and teachers. Weekend church conferences, led by informed Christian laymen who are scientists would allow the issue to be drawn with viewpoints represented fairly. Laymen could then fairly judge whether a person can be a professing Christian and interested in the results of scientific research and whether science and religion really contradict or indeed complement each other.

It is a rare issue of *The Plain Truth* magazine which does

not have an article on science and evolution. Unfortunately, science is constantly condemned as delving into the things of God. One such statement is as follows: "For thousands of years mankind has lived according to this philosophy of trial and error. He has continually sought knowledge by experimentation alone. He has continually rejected revelation from any god and attempted to 'play God.' "[24] Evangelical Christians can retain an interest in science while maintaining faith in the creative power of God.

From the Worldwide Church of God and other Adventists, evangelical Christians can learn anew the obvious meaning of the phrase, "It is later now than it has ever been." Regardless of how one may feel toward those who would predict the coming of Christ within this decade, it is evident that Jesus' coming "is nearer than when we first believed." This can add a sense of urgency to the church's mission task. The first-century church grew rapidly partly because it was convinced that Jesus would soon return. Modern evangelical Christians appear to be not so convinced.

The Anglo-Israel movement points up the crucial need for intense and intelligent Bible study. This includes a thorough and scholarly study of biblical prophecy, led by informed pastors. As evangelical Christians are led to further truth by intelligent reading of the Bible, fewer will be led away by those who promise overdrawn analyses of the world tomorrow.

The Worldwide Church of God, with its consistent emphasis on the production of quality radio and television programs and magazines, is evidence of how a religious group can grow primarily through use of the mass media. Oral Roberts and Billy Graham have demonstrated the effectiveness of quality religious programing. Other evangelical groups may take note.

How to Witness

This author has found that in witnessing to members of the Worldwide Church of God, love and stressing of the grace of God is most important. Patience is a quality needed in dealing with devotees of the Armstrongs, because these are often persons convinced of their brand of truth.

One proven technique is to introduce the followers of Anglo-Israelism to other methods of Bible interpretation. On occasion this author has purchased a one-volume Bible commentary for the new friend to whom he is witnessing. A method which has helped also is a verse-by-verse exegesis of Paul's letter to the Galatians, majoring on the relation of law and gospel. These methods are effective only when both parties are interested not in winning arguments, but in finding truth.

Chapter IV

CHRISTIAN SCIENCE: HEALING OR HOAX

The founder of Christian Science, Mrs. Mary Baker Eddy, once wrote, "The opponents of Christian Science must be charitable, if they be Christian."[1] This author has sought to be charitable in writing this chapter and hesitates even to be classified as an "opponent" of Christian Science. When viewed objectively, Christian Science must be seen as a healer to millions who have discovered in it a type of positive thinking which helps them function in an age of anxiety. However, Christian Science differs doctrinally and creates a wide gap between itself and evangelical Christianity.

New Thought

Christian Science is part of a wider pattern of religious faith and practice in the world known properly as New Thought. Books by Dale Carnegie, Norman Vincent Peale, and James Allen strongly emphasize the presuppositions of New Thought.

New Thought, as a philosophical movement, originated in the nineteenth century. It may be defined as "the fine art of recognizing, realizing, and manifesting the God in the individual." Julius A. Dresser and Annetta Seabury were the first to organize effectively what has since been called New Thought. They learned a great deal from Phineas P. Quimby, who taught that God is omnipresent wisdom.

Quimby fought constantly against priests and doctors, and equated his science with truth.

The main teachings of New Thought may be summarized as follows:

1. Ideals are realities and internal forces are primary causes.
2. Mind is primary and causative, while matter is secondary.
3. Men are the spiritual citizens of a divine universe.
4. The remedy for all defect and disorder is metaphysical.
5. God is immanent.
6. Humanity is divine.
7. Truth is present and revealed progressively to every new generation.
8. Man can be free from the necessity of belief in disease.
9. Man's real search is the discovery of his own soul.
10. Evil has no place in the plan of God.
11. There is no future punishment, as in hell.[2]

New Thought's premises may be summarized as follows: Every man has a right and responsibility to live his own life in accordance with the highest dictates of his own conscience with mind always expanding and reaching out for a better definition of itself.

New Thought is more of a point of view than a discernible religious movement. It may appear in a Christian Science testimony meeting or in the latest copy of *Guideposts* magazine. There will always be some people who perceive of religious experience primarily as deliverance for *them*, with little accompanying desire for redemptive social involvement. Positive thinking will always have its advocates. Its ability to permeate a society's religious thought patterns is evident in America.

Unity School of Christianity

This author visited Unity Farm at Lee's Summit, Missouri, in 1971, and was very cordially received. James Freeman, director of the Department of Silent Unity, was giving a lecture. He said, "Unity was founded by Charles and Myrtle Filmore. He had come from an Episcopal background and was in the real estate business in Kansas City. Myrtle was a Methodist who was constantly ill until they both met a Dr. Weeks who came to them from the Illinois Metaphysical Seminary. Dr. Weeks taught the couple that one does not inherit sickness." Mr. Freeman continued, "Unity really began as a prayer and healing movement. Having been healed, the Filmores started a magazine named *Modern Thought*. In 1912 Charles Filmore wrote his first book, *Christian Healing.*"

Mr. Freeman then turned to Unity in the present tense, "Ours is an open-ended religion, the religion of the free mind. In Silent Unity, a service of prayer for others, we answer a million and a half letters a month. We average receiving 140,000 phone calls per week. We teach people in trouble that God is good and that he is in every person. Actually, we represent joy in religion, trying to get man to reach his unlimited potential."

During the time of questions and answers, Mr. Freeman was asked what Unity students believe about Jesus. The reply was, "Jesus was our elder brother. As the 'Way Shower,' Jesus' life was a great example for us. Jesus taught us how to lift the human up to the Divine. Jesus Christ is now here raising me to his consciousness of life. He is the man we all might be. Jesus is perfect love."

The lecture was over but the curiosity of this author was only beginning to be stimulated. Further research revealed that Unity headquarters employs more than five hundred people. More than four and a half-million pieces of literature go out from Unity headquarters every month.

Further research on Unity teaching reveals close parallels with Christian Science. One sentence summarizes the Unity view, "Unity teaches that the Spirit of God dwells within man, that God is ever seeking to renew and to heal man's mind, body, and affairs, and that His will for man is always good."[3]

One of Unity's most popular publications is *Wee Wisdom,* which carries the subtitle, "A Character-Building for Boys and Girls." The center-fold of a recent issue summed up Unity thought for children, "I live in a good world. My good thoughts and good feelings add up to the good all around me."[4]

New is an increasingly popular magazine for adults which recently carried an article on Southern Baptist Anita Bryant. She was quoted on the subject of prayer, "Strength is not in ourselves, strength comes from God. And if you pray, you will receive strength and will be guided."[5]

Unity is not to be confused with Christian Science, although both are in the general category of New Thought. A Unity minister, Bernard Dozier makes this clear in the following statements on Unity:

   4. It has no creedal requirements; . . .
  20. Believes no negative condition of mind, body, or affairs is incurable.
  21. Teaches and demonstrates that healing comes through believing prayer, but accepts all forms of healing as divine. . . .
  34. Accepts the Bible as its basic textbook of truth, and believes the Scriptures represent the testimonies of men who perceived much truth. . . .[6]

Unity and Christian Science have in common the basic viewpoints of New Thought but differ on some points. Unity recognizes that sin, evil, and death are realities to be coped with. Unity sees the Bible as a basic textbook without need of supplement from *Science and Health* or other inspired writings. Further, Unity is not as concerned with establishing local congregations as is Christian Science.

Unity will probably continue to attract many within Christian churches despite its schizophrenic view of Jesus Christ. Unity claims to have faith in Christ but not in Jesus the man as being divine. Self-deification is an option because of this split view of Jesus Christ. Elizabeth Sand Turner wrote: "We acknowledge Jesus as the way-shower of the race, and we believe that by following his commandments we can bring into full expression of our own divine nature, the Christ, and eventually regenerate the body as he did."[7] A low Christology among Unity students should slow its growth. However, only the informed among evangelical Christians can detect the unorthodox teachings being perpetuated by the Unity School.

Christian Science

Christian Science has grown from fewer than fifty thousand in 1900 to more than four hundred thousand adherents in 1972. It is a respected movement in most major metropolitan areas in the world. Reading rooms and a well-known newspaper, *The Christian Science Monitor,* keep this thought pattern before the public. It probably will continue to proselyte from churches those members who have not found in them a sufficient ministry to their emotional needs, and those who are ill-informed on their faith. Many who are attracted to Christian Science's healing power are unaware of its history.

Christian Science is inseparable from the career of one Mary Baker Eddy. She was born to Congregationalist parents in 1821 in Bern, New Hampshire. As a child, she was a victim of frequent illness and melancholy. She was first married at age twenty-two to one George Glover. Mr. Glover died only seven months later, leaving his pregnant bride alone to bear George, Jr. Nine years later Mrs. Glover married a dentist, Dr. Daniel Patterson. Their marriage ended in divorce several months after he abandoned her in 1866. Her third marriage was in 1877 to Asa Eddy, the first of her pupils to announce publicly that he was a Christian Science practitioner. Mr. Eddy's death in 1882 came as a harsh blow to his devoted wife who charged in local newspapers that he had been killed by arsenic which was "mentally administered."

The degree of Mary Baker Eddy's reliance for her ideas on Dr. Phineas P. Quimby remains a subject of lively debate. Most are agreed on the outline of her contacts with him. As Mrs. Patterson, she first went to be treated by Quimby in October of 1862 in Portland, Maine. She was impressed with his contention that the Bible contained a hidden science to solve life's problems. She stayed on a few weeks to aid Dr. Quimby in treating his patients. She later denied any reliance on Quimby for her ideas on the science of healing. However, Horatio W. Dresser published a work which contained correspondence between her and Quimby, which verified her dependence on him.[8]

Phineas P. Quimby died in January, 1866. An event the following month was regarded by Mrs. Eddy as the turning point in her life. She fell on an icy pavement and spent three pain-filled days in her bed until she was healed as she read Matthew 9:2–8, the story of the healing by Jesus of the man afflicted with palsy. She vowed to spend the rest of her life emphasizing the healing power in religion. The next nine years were filled with disappointment and intense study.

A major milestone in the Christian Science came in 1875 with the publication of *Science and Health with Key to the Scriptures*. In 1879 a charter was obtained and the Church of Christ, Scientist, was organized in Boston, and Mrs. Eddy was called as pastor. Two years later the training of Christian Scientists was started in the Massachusetts Metaphysical College. The publication of the *Christian Science Journal* was started in 1883. The next year Mrs. Eddy went to Chicago to give a series of lectures to her followers there, evidence that the movement was spreading. In 1886 the National Scientist Association was organized.

Mrs. Eddy retired from active local leadership in 1889 and moved to Concord, New Hampshire. Five years later the First Church of Christ, Scientist, was built at a cost of a quarter million dollars in Boston. It is frequently referred to as the Mother Church. By 1894 there were over five thousand members of the movement located in thirty-seven states. In 1908 Mrs. Eddy founded *The Christian Science Monitor,* a daily newspaper which currently has over half a million subscribers and emphasizes what is "right with people in the news."

Since Mrs. Eddy's death in 1910, no other person has served as pastor of the Mother Church. The movement continues to rely heavily on her influences and writings, and is led by a board of directors, which was declared in 1921 by the Supreme Judicial Court of Massachusetts to be the final authority in the Christian Science Church.

The growth of Christian Science has leveled off in recent years. The future of the movement is difficult to predict. Nonetheless, widespread use of mass advertising, the image of intellectual astuteness projected by the *Monitor,* tales of healing by such celebrities as Doris Day and Alan Young, and the prominent use of reading rooms will probably cause Christian Science to grow numerically on the religious scene.

A Question of Revelation

Science and Health with Key to the Scriptures is a second scripture to the Christian Scientists. This is clear in the constant use of it and the authority accorded to it. Actually, it is treated as equal to or greater than the Bible, since the true meaning of the Bible supposedly comes through the divine interpretation given it in *Science and Health*. An exclusive magazine recently carried a full-page ad urging readers to purchase a copy of the main textbook of Christian Science. The ad presented the book as presenting "an entirely fresh look at the teachings of Christ Jesus" and revealing "the true spiritual significance" of the Bible's content.[9]

Most Christian Scientists would assert that Mrs. Eddy's teachings came through direct revelation from God to their leader. Other students of American intellectual history of a century ago might point to a general climate of thought in her day which had direct influence on her. Not the least of these influences was that of New Thought, which relies heavily on emphasizing the spiritual aspects of life as opposed to the evil material world. Man was thought to be basically divine by leading philosophers of the day, such as Ralph Waldo Emerson. Some elements of Hindu philosophy were prevalent in Mrs. Eddy's day, such as the secondary importance of matter and emphasis on the oneness of all reality.

Mary Baker Eddy was largely self-educated and could hardly have bypassed the intellectual currents of her day. She recorded that in her youth her favorite studies were "natural philosophy, logic and moral science."[10] It appears to most objective observers of Christian Science that her readings, coupled with an imaginative mind, were factors in Mrs. Eddy's development of thought.

Mrs. Eddy was aware that she lived in a time of intellectual ferment. She wrote in the preface to *Science and Health,* "The time for thinkers has come. Truth, independent of doctrines and time-honored systems, knocks at the portals of humanity."[11] Though she knew her ideas were new to most Christians, Mrs. Eddy at least tried to tie her teachings to the Bible. She wrote, "Divine science derives its sanction from the Bible."[12] Yet, she contended that God's revelation to her was more final than the Bible itself, "God had been graciously preparing me during many years for the reception of this final revelation of the absolute divine principle of scientific mental healing."[13] Further, the founder of Christian Science called for a more "advanced" way to read the Bible: "The literal rendering of the Scriptures makes them nothing valuable, but often is the foundation of unbelief and hopelessness. The metaphysical rendering is health and peace and hope for all."[14]

Even more important for the modern student is the question of how Christian Scientists today view the revelation to their leader. At least one modern spokesman for Mrs. Eddy's followers is willing to write this, "The revelation of divine science was a divine revelation to Mrs. Eddy. . . . The divine revelation took the form of Science and Health."[15] Mrs. Eddy herself considered her revelation to be of divine significance: "The second appearing of Jesus is, unquestionably, the spiritual advent of the advancing idea of God, as in Christian Science."[16]

Most Christian Scientists today regard their founder as the supreme and final channel of revelation. The church she founded is careful to protect her memory from unfavorable publicity. Evangelical Christians regard as heretical this tendency to canonize Mrs. Eddy's writings and to idealize her person as they do any attempt to supplement the Scriptures with a disclosure of "hidden" meaning. This tendency is also heretical, especially in those instances where it replaces classical Christian statements of the nature of man and God with metaphysical interpretations. The manner in which this is done is examined in the next section.

Doctrines

For evangelical Christians, the most important question in doctrine is the one relating to salvation. Mrs. Eddy defines salvation as, "Life, truth and love understood and demonstrated as supreme over all; sin, sickness and death destroyed."[17] She is narrow on the manner of salvation, "There is but one way to heaven, harmony and Christ in divine science shows us this way. It is to know no other reality . . . than good, God and his reflection."[18] For Christian Science, salvation means deliverance from any awareness of evil or pain and the enjoyment of only the wholesome and positive elements of life.

In Christian Science doctrine, sin is error and is to be conquered by denying its power or existence. The death of Christ makes little or no difference in the matter of individual salvation, according to Mrs. Eddy. She wrote, "Man as God's idea is already saved with an everlasting salvation."[19]

Most Christians can hardly recognize the doctrine of God as taught by Christian Science. The founder of the movement wrote to her followers, "Life, truth and love constitute the triune person called God. . . . God the father-mother, Christ, the spiritual idea of sonship; divine science or the holy comforter."[20] God is in no sense a person for the Christian Scientist, but a principle.

A most serious gap between Christian Science thought and classic Christian statements of faith comes at the point of the person and nature of Jesus Christ. The Christian Science textbook states clearly, "a portion of God could not enter man; neither could God's fulness be reflected by a single man."[21] As in the case of Unity, the historical Jesus and the Christ are not used in Christian Science as synonymous. Jesus was not divine, but only the Christ principle in him was true deity. Jesus is merely the name of the man who presented this principle better than anyone else. He was supposedly endowed with the divine "Christ-spirit" without measure. In the final analysis, this doctrine denies the necessity for the incarnation of God and the deity of Jesus.

Christian Science does not stress Jesus' physical resurrection. Mrs. Eddy even denied that Jesus ever died. She wrote, "Jesus' students did not perform many wonderful works until they saw him after his crucifixion and learned that he had not died."[22]

The chief postulates of the Christian Science may be summarized as follows: life is good; spirit cannot be limited to matter; life is not subject to death or evil; and the really spiritual man has no material life or death.

A Critical Analysis

There are some similarities between Christian Science thought and evangelical Christian statements of faith. Both agree that God is all-powerful as the Creator and is good. Both assert that while Jesus was on earth he healed multiple types of diseases. However, the differences in belief far outweigh the similarities. Only three of these key differences are treated here.

One key dissimilarity is the view and use of the Bible. Mrs. Eddy wrote, "The material record of the Bible is no more important to our well-being than the history of Europe and America."[23] While evangelical Christians rely heavily on a rather literal view of the Bible for their doctrines, Christian Scientists prefer to have the "hidden" meaning in the Bible speak to them. A significant example of this use of Scripture is seen in Mrs. Eddy's "proof" that the Holy Spirit is really Divine Science, "In the words of Saint John, 'He shall give you another comforter, that he may abide with you forever.' This comforter I understand to be divine science."[24]

A second major divergent is evident on the matter of man in relation to evil or negative realities, i.e., sin, illness, and death. Mrs. Eddy put her thought simply, "Man is incapable of sin, sickness and death."[25] First John 1:10 states the biblical view of man just as clearly, "If we say that we have not sinned, we make a liar out of God, and his word is not in us."

Christian Science, thirdly, refuses to admit the reality of sickness in the human order. Mrs. Eddy wrote, "Sin, disease and death have no foundation in truth."[26] In other contexts, Christian Scientists are taught that man is never sick and that no maladies such as nervous breakdowns or dislocated bones can occur in reality. Jesus, in Matthew 11, spoke of a different view of disease, "Go show John again those things which you do hear and see: the blind receive their sight, and the lame walk . . . and the deaf hear, the dead are raised up. . . ."

A critical analysis of Christian Science revolves around their unrealistic view of the negative but redeemable qualities of life. Evangelized Christians offer a realistic view of man being basically sinful but redeemable through the grace of God. Death is faced realistically with no attempt to deny its stark power. Evil is seen as rampant force ultimately under the providence of God. Hope comes through facing reality with confident faith. Need for denial vanishes.

Social Concern

Christian Science has as its ultimate goal the making of individuals who have found peace within. A dominant factor in the enlisting of new adult converts by Christian Science is the healing ministry. Every issue of the *Christian Science Sentinel* and the *Christian Science Journal* contains testimonies of healings. As do most of the mind healing groups, Christian Science stresses the removal of disease by the thinking of pure thoughts. This is often aided by the reading of *Science and Health* or the consulting of a practitioner. The practitioner instructs the patient how to overcome his illness by refusing to think of it.

There is little doubt that Christian Science performs a valuable service to society by ministering to many who are emotionally disturbed and whose diseases are induced by suggestion. However, there is little medical documentation of the cures since verification comes almost totally from within Christian Science circles. Christian Science practitioners have won the legal right to practice in most states, despite repeated protests from medical doctors, and continue to practice healing on those who desire their type of assistance.

The pursuing of the goal of individual healing does not lend itself to collective social action. Since Christian Science regards evil and sin as but illusions, a sure sign of a lack of faith is to become overly concerned about them. As a result, Christian Scientists have shown little interest in lessening interracial tensions or in building educational institutions except those which specifically teach their system of thought. Unlike most alternative groups, Christian Scientists do not sponsor a structured foreign missionary effort. One negative aspect of Christian Science is that it does not encourage redemptive social action. Whether healing or hoax, Christian Science continues to minister to a population segment which some evangelical Christians ignore.

What They Can Teach Us

The fact that there are now over a third of a million Christian Scientists in the United States, despite their deviant doctrine, is an indication that some lessons can be learned from them by evangelical Christians.

First, the fact that Christian Science grows primarily on the basis of mind healing is due partially to the fact that other religious groups fail to offer full programs of counseling. Jesus' pattern of ministry revealed his interest in the complete personality. To follow seriously in his example will necessitate for evangelical Christians an increased emphasis on the training of more pastors as counselors, the utilization of community resources for the mentally ill and disturbed and the genuine active concern of the Christian community for the emotionally ill.

A second lesson evangelical Christians can learn from Christian Science is the power of the written word. The daily newspaper, *The Christian Science Monitor,* has received numerous prizes for reporting, and it gives to the public an image of intellectual integrity for the whole movement. Christian Science reading rooms are noticeable in every major metropolitan area, a witnessing approach which others might well emulate.

A third lesson evangelical Christians might well learn from Christian Science is the emphasis that religious thought permeates all of life. Every attitude and action is part of discipleship. Salvation is not an isolated aspect of living.

How to Witness to a Christian Scientist

Any effort to witness must be supported by the twin powers of prayer and the power of the Holy Spirit. A basic knowledge of Christian Science history and doctrines is helpful. The Christian Scientist should be aware that the interest is in him as a person. This may require months of cultivation and demonstration evangelism in which he is able to observe, in the evangelical Christian he sees, a sense of peace which comes by acknowledging (not denying or ignoring) one's disharmony with God.

Frank discussion of the nature of biblical authority should be interspersed with the mutual study of Scripture, with special emphasis on those passages dealing with the nature of man, sin, death, and the resurrection. One-to-one Bible studies are helpful in witnessing, with careful and patient attention given to definition of terms.

If Christian Scientists can see Christlike concern in the witness' faith, peace of mind in forgiveness of sin, and an open-minded searching of Scripture, he may be led to search for that same faith and be led to rest his life on Jesus Christ in his deity.

Chapter V

THE BLACK MUSLIMS AND ELIJAH (POOLE) MUHAMMAD

Charles Silberman in *Crisis in Black and White* argued that the Negro's color and "previously condition of servitude" (as the old books called slavery) made all the difference between him and other immigrants. Silberman said that black people are characterized by "despair and apathy," hatred of white people, self-hatred, and the lack of personal and collective identity.[1]

Nowhere are the characteristics described by Dr. Silberman more apparent than in the Black Muslim movement. As much a sociological and psychological reaction to "white" Christianity as a religious movement, the Black Muslims draw growth response from the Negro population by preaching isolation and segregation from the whites. Collective identity as a people is offered offended blacks in the name of an African religion which can be said to be distinctively black.

Rap Brown, Stokely Carmichael, Eldridge Cleaver, Angela Davis, and other advocates of radical Black Power have come and gone off the American civil rights scene. The Black Muslims have been a steadily growing manifestation of black consciousness. This is despite doctrines which sound strange to Christian ears, black or white:

A great deal of what the Bible prophetically teaches of Messenger Elijah Muhammad is erroneously thought to refer to the Jesus of 2000 years ago. . . . Messenger Muhammad has shown us in

71

the Scriptures all the prophecies that are fulfilled in our eyes today. If we accept all of what he has so clearly taught us, we cannot help but also see those parts of the total prophetic sayings that
show who the Messenger Muhammad is, his unique position with
Allah and the rest of human life, his sublime character—in short,
his divinity.[2]

This assertion about the deity of Elijah Muhammad, the
Black Muslim leader, is just one among many doctrines
and doctrines which may sound strange to most American
Christians. However, the Black Muslim movement is already nationwide and is growing rapidly with at least 220,-
000 members. C. Eric Lincoln points out that only Billy
Graham has attracted and converted more people in recent
years than has Elijah Muhammad.[3] When Muhammad
speaks, his crowds often range into the tens of thousands.
The weekly radio program, "Muhammad Speaks," is heard
on at least forty radio stations covering more than fifteen
major metropolitan areas. Regular Muslim meetings are
currently held in almost eighty temples across the nation.

With the conversion of Cassius Clay, the Black Muslims
have received national publicity for their movement, which
combines social protest and religious fervor. The future
of the movement is dependent on the speed with which
white America and black America resolve their difficulties.

The articulate Christian witness should be informed and
alert to the growth of the movement in order to understand
and minister to both these Muslims and those persons only
loosely related to the saving Son of God, whether in the
white or black community.

Brief History

In 1929 W. D. Farad came to the black community of
Detroit and began to speak about what he called the true
religion of the black man. He soon began to attract large

crowds and leased a hall which he called the Temple of Islam. Farad claimed to be from Mecca and to have the mission of introducing his black race to the Koran. He taught his followers that white men were "blue-eyed devils" who were vicious deceivers. Mr. Farad, the self-proclaimed "Supreme Ruler of the Universe," put some of his writings into a book entitled *Teaching for the Lost Found Nation of Islam in a Mathematical Way*.

One of Farad's early converts was Elijah Poole. Mr. Poole is the son of a black Baptist minister and was born in Sandersville, Georgia. He saw his father lynched by an angry mob. He then fled to Chicago, where he met W. D. Farad. Elijah (Poole) Muhammad is now more than seventy-five years of age but is still the powerful force behind the Black Muslims. He is called the Messenger of Allah and has been personally responsible for the spread of the movement.

Farad disappeared in 1934 after attracting some eight thousand followers. Elijah Muhammad has given the movement stable leadership since then and has been instrumental in making it a business-religion establishment, acquiring schools, hotels, restaurants, land, and the University of Islam in Chicago.

Elijah Muhammad came to Chicago in 1932 and established what was to be called Temple of Islam Number 2. When Farad disappeared, Muhammad proclaimed his mosque the new headquarters of the movement. He said that Farad was to be called the "Savior" and his birthday, February 26, is celebrated by the Muslims as "Savior's Day."

In 1961, C. Eric Lincoln, author of a standard work on the Muslims, predicted that young Malcolm X would logically be the successor of Elijah.[4] Facts have evolved otherwise. Malcolm X broke with the Black Muslims in 1964 to change to true Islam and was assassinated a year later. The last month he was alive he tried to buy a Harlem church to establish an orthodox Muslim mosque. He has become a folk hero to black militants. *Newsweek* quotes one of his admirers as saying, "There were no black students before Malcolm died—there were only Negroes."[5]

Regardless of the identity of the man named soon to succeed Elijah Muhammad, the Black Muslim movement owes its durability and form to the one they call the Messenger of Allah. It is more than coincidence that the Muslim newspaper is entitled *Muhammad Speaks*.

Muslim Doctrines

Twelve articles of faith constitute the section which invariably appears on the back page of *Muhammad Speaks* under the title, "What the Muslims Believe." They are as follows:

1. WE BELIEVE in the One God Whose proper Name is Allah.
2. . . . in the Holy Qur-an and in the Scriptures of all the Prophets of God.
3. . . . in the truth of the Bible, but we believe that it has been tampered with and must be reinterpreted so that mankind will not be snared by the falsehoods that have been added to it.
4. . . . in Allah's Prophets and the Scriptures they brought to the people.
5. . . . in the resurrection of the dead—not in physical resurrection—but in mental resurrection. . . . Furthermore, we believe we are the people of God's choice. . . .
6. . . . in the judgement; we believe this first judgement will take place as God revealed, in America. . . .
7. . . . this is the time in history for the separation of the so-called Negroes and the so-called white Americans. . . .
8. . . . in justice for all, whether in God or not. . . .
9. . . . that the offer of integration is hypocritical. . . .
10. . . . that we who declared ourselves to be righteous Muslims, should not participate in wars which take the lives of humans. . . .

11. . . . our women should be respected and protected as the women of other nationalities are respected and protected.
12. . . . That Allah (God) appeared in the Person of Master W. Farad Muhammad, July, 1930; the long-awaited "Messiah" of the Christians and the "Mahdi" of the Muslims. . . .[6]

Theologically, it is apparent that the Black Muslim movement qualifies as a deviation from both Christianity and Islam. As reflected in articles 2 and 3, there is a tendency to affirm the Koran and relate it to the Bible. Christ is not mentioned in this creed, while W. Farad Muhammad is proclaimed as both "Messiah" of the Christians and "Mahdi" of the Muslims. Article 5 is indicative of black identity under the title of God's people. Article 6 is a veiled vindictive statement that God's judgment will be poured out first on sinful America.

Elijah Muhammad claims that he knows Allah and that he is with him. Further, all black men are representatives of Allah, and Allah is the name of the Supreme Being among a mighty nation of divine black men. When asked on a television interview whether he taught that all members of Islam are God and that Allah is supreme, Elijah Muhammad responded, "That's right."[7] The black man is held to be divine by his very nature and supposedly all "so-called Negroes" are Muslims. The black man is also original man: creator of the universe and primogenitor of all other races, even the white race for which a special method of birth control was used.

Christ is seen as a Muslim prophet who spoke often through parables about Negroes. Elijah Muhammed has written that Jesus was "only a prophet and not the equal of Moses and Muhammad, and that his religion was Islam, and not the Christianity of the Pope of Rome."[8] Christianity is consistently viewed by the Black Muslims as the white man's religion. The "blue-eyed devils" are to be identified with Satan, and their rule over the earth ended in 1914.[9] Elijah Muhammad wrote in a booklet entitled "The Supreme Wisdom" that "Christianity is a religion organized and backed by the devils for the purpose of making slaves of black mankind."[10] As is evident, the Black Muslim theology has evolved from a negative reaction to "white" Christianity.

According to Muhammad, Jesus experienced no resurrection and made no promises regarding heaven and hell. "There is no heaven or hell other than on earth for you and me, and Jesus was no exception. His body is still . . . in Palestine and will remain there."[11] So, the fact of the physical resurrection of Christ suffers from an overreaction to hypocritical Christianity.

Doctrinally, the Black Muslims' thought patterns reflect a radical reaction against a pseudo-Christianity. The "Christianity" against which they rebel makes the following subconscious or conscious assumptions:

1. God is primarily concerned about the world to come. This world can be endured if enough is said and believed about heaven for the faithful.
2. God has decreed that certain colored races are inferior and to be servants of the white race.
3. The resurrection of Christ is the basis for a hope for the future which salves "open sores" of the present.
4. White American Christians are God's chosen people, to be honored with blessings and luxuries as well as responsibility.
5. The Christian ideals of love and justice are impossible goals to be talked about much and practiced little.

The type of Christianity against which Muhammad's followers react is a far cry from the biblical witness or from Christian discipleship as described in the introduction to this book. This type of "white" Christianity is itself an alternative to discipleship as described in the New Testament. It overlooks the complementary balance between the present and coming kingdom of heaven, the equality of races which Jesus personified with the Samaritans much to the chagrin of the strict Jews of his day, that the message of the resurrection is as much a guide to current living as to future hope, that covenant calling involves being open to people of every race, and that the teachings of Jesus are hard yet practical demands for kingdom living. The Christianity against which the Muslims react is but a poor perversion of Christ's example and teaching. Perhaps the evident growing presence of the Black Muslims will serve as a call to reformation within the folk religion which passes for Christianity in some instances.

As to whether the Black Muslims are a part of mainstream Islam or a deviate sect, opinion differs strongly. C. Eric Lincoln's view of the question is that Black Muslims differ from the orthodox Moslems in two key areas: the belief that it is the destiny of the black nation to inherit the earth and the idea that the black man must separate himself from the white race.[12] Mainstream Moslem groups in the United States have refused to recognize these Muslims as being within Islam, although on a tour in 1959, Malcolm X was received by the leaders of the Moslem Congress.

In summary, the movement led by Elijah Muhammad is such a reaction against the Christianity it has encountered and so fervently proclaims the divine nature of the black man that it does not as yet emerge as a Moslem sect but as a Christian deviation, i.e., more of a social and doctrinally reactionary group than a movement within Islam.

Muslim Morals

Dr. Harry Edwards of San Jose State College studied fourteen black Christian homes and fourteen Black Muslim homes and made the following observations:

1. Most of the Muslim men were employed while most of the Christian men were unemployed.
2. The Muslim couples would not permit anyone to smoke, drink or curse in their homes.
3. The Muslim couples had children in frequent, stairstep progression which reflected their total rejection of all methods of birth control.
4. The Nation of Islam gives assistance toward economic self-sufficiency with membership.
5. Muslim women confide only in their husbands.[13]

All Muslims are forbidden to overeat, drink liquor, smoke or gamble, and the men are urged to hold steady jobs. Many ex-prisoners, drug addicts, alcoholics, and prostitutes are welcomed into the movement for a type of personal rehabilitation. They are expected to pray five times a day, as are all Moslems. Pork is forbidden, and Elijah Muhammad persistently insists that one meal a day is sufficient. Most copies of *Muhammad Speaks* carry several articles on the health message of the Black Muslims, ranging in topics from breastfeeding to abstinence from pork.

Muslim women are urged to be careful not to allow opportunity for sexual promiscuity. They are not allowed to be in any room alone without their husband. They are also instructed to be obedient to their husband.

The Black Muslims' austerity in personal morals is, unfortunately, mingled with radical racism which can produce hatred. An example of this attitude is recorded in an editorial in the Muslim newspaper:

We are all racists who have two cents worth of knowledge, because racism is only the love of your own race. But, you love other than your own race, and you want to join in and love everybody. This is your damnation, Mr. Preacher; because everybody is not to be loved. It is only the righteous who are to be loved.[14]

The Black Muslims have succeeded in doing precisely what they justifiably have said many Christians do, they have combined a set of doctrines, personal pietism, and racial hatred. Settlement between the races will hardly be affected by either group without exposure to each other. Man fails to find God in his fulness unless he finds his fellowman. While there is ample justification for black assertion of pride, both groups must differentiate in attitude between self-respect and hatred.

Commendable individual piety and high morals does help reclaim individual lives, but concerted effort must be given to the atonement of races, a task hardly to be attempted or completed when accompained by racial hatred.

Muslim Wants

A Muslim minister summed up the aims of his movement when he said, "To get the white man's foot off my neck, his hand out of my pocket and his carcass off my back. To sleep in my own bed without fear and to look straight into his cold blue eyes and call him a liar every time he parts his lips."[15]

An entirely separate black economy is projected as one tool for achieving the goals listed above. The Muslims operate department stores, barber shops, restaurants, and grocery stores in many major cities in the United States. Income from the various enterprises exceeds $1.6 million annually and efforts are expanding. Frequent ads call for qualified management personnel who are clean-cut, regardless of their relation to the Muslim faith. Solicitations are often made for "true and sincere experienced black farmers" to work farm lands owned by the group.

Elijah Muhammad lists ten things the Muslims want:

1. We want freedom. . . .
2. . . . justice. . . .
3. . . . equality of opportunity. . . .
4. . . . our people in America . . . to be allowed to establish a separate state or territory of their own—either on this continent or elsewhere. . . .

5. . . . freedom for all Believers of Islam now held in federal prison. . . .
6. . . . an immediate end to the police brutality and attacks against the so-called Negro throughout the United States. . . .
7. . . . we demand not only equal justice under the laws of the United States, but equal employment opportunities—NOW! . . .
8. . . . the government of the United States to exempt our people from ALL taxation as long as we are deprived of equal justice under the laws of the land. . . .
9. . . . equal education. . . . all black children educated, taught and trained by their own teachers. . . .
10. . . . intermarriage or race mixing should be prohibited. . . . the religion of Islam taught without hinderance or suppression.[16]

A consistent demand reflected in the list alone is for land for the black man. Demands have ranged up to seven states to be called their own. Occasional threats also come that the black man will flee en masse to another nation or continent, leaving the white men devoid of a large labor force. Some large tracts of lands are being bought by the Muslims, using the title of the Progressive Land Development Corporation of Chicago, the president of which is a Mr. Aharrief, a son-in-law of Elijah Muhammad.

An example of this consistent quest for land is the endorsement of the efforts of the National Democratic Party, headed by Dr. John Cashin, to assume political control of a strip of fifteen counties across the south central tip of Alabama. Dr. Cashin has said, "The Honorable Elijah Muhammad is the best person I can think of capable of developing the land in Alabama as a model for black people."[17]

The pronouncements regarding separate education are also reflective of the desire for segregation of the black man—supposedly providing opportunity for the total development of the race in Islam.

Muslim Worship

Black Muslim mosques are usually located in the center of the black community, sometimes in abandoned churches or synagogues left vacant by whites who have left a racially changing community. Whites are never allowed in temple services. Arabic phrases are very much a part of the ceremony, with each participant expected to learn familiar greetings.

Each lecture hall displays one painting—divided between the signs of Islam and the signs of Christianity. The signs of Islam are a star and crescent with the words, "Freedom—Justice—Equality." The signs of Christianity are depicted as the Christian cross, an American flag, and a black man hanging by his neck from a tree. This supposedly depicts the choice in religion for the American black man.

The focus of the temple service is a long oratory by the local or visiting minister. The address may last more than two hours and usually covers a wide range of subjects, from economics to Christianity to personal chastity. An opportunity is given at the end of the service for those who would "declare for Islam." These worship services are part of a conscious attempt to create a mystique of hope for the black community.

What They Can Teach Us

C. Eric Lincoln characterizes the typical Black Muslim as a young, economically lower-class, male American Negro who is a common laborer.[18] He may very well be a former nominal Methodist or Baptist—more than 80 percent are. The basic appeal of most Black Power movements is to the lower economic classes, to men and women who have little place to go except up. They are attracted to any group which will give them group identity and self-respect. This could be given by evangelical Christian churches fulfilling their total mission in discipleship—including projects such as the credit union run by Wheat Street Baptist Church in Atlanta.

Evangelical Christians would do well to emulate the zeal behind the evangelistic methods employed by the Muslims. As with many of the alternative groups, they have learned the value of public relations and employ the best spokesmen for their faith. Well-dressed, polite, and soft-spoken Muslim men are enlisted to distribute literature near churches on Sunday morning. Their sense of urgency is commendable, if not their timing.

C. Eric Lincoln asks an embarassing question of Christians, "Shall we expect any other religion, even Islam to be more insistent on brotherly love than we are ourselves?"[19] Black brothers can be reached for Christ when Christians learn to love all people enough to seek justice for them.

There are several lessons to be learned, even from a movement which is doctrinally a combination of Islamic and anti-Christian credal statements.

How to Witness to Black Muslims

The Christian witness to the Black Muslims must include several essential steps:

1. The restoration of the image of Christianity as "culture-shattering" and not merely "culture-reflecting." Jesus preached a revolutionary ethic which is to be followed by his disciples with its subsequent judgment of society.

2. A second step in witnessing to the Black Muslim is the support and training of the black Christian minister on an equal basis. The training of black Christian prison chaplains is of top priority status in this witnessing endeavor. Black Muslims are very active in most federal prisons.

The Christ-event stands on its own merit when explained by a clear and Christian witness. Unfortunately, some of the rejection of the message of Christ has been caused by the witness being loud about God and quiet about brotherly love.

Frequently, in conversation with Black Muslims, this author

asks the blunt question of whether the two communities, black and white, can achieve social justice in the long run by remaining segregated. A good lead question is, "What will American society be like by the year 2000 if black and white Americans remain isolated from each other?"

Chapter VI

EAST IS EAST AND WEST IS . . . AFFECTED

Rudyard Kipling, in the *Ballad of East and West,* wrote a beautiful stanza which is often quoted:

> Oh, East is East, and West is West,
> and never the twain shall meet,
> Til Earth and Sky stand presently at
> God's great Judgment Seat. . . .

Kipling's observation that East will never meet West is a good addition to a masterpiece of poetry but is an inaccurate statement regarding the contemporary scene in America today and Western Christian thought has been affected radically.

The youth subculture has been molded by what is basic Buddhist thought. Such phrases as "do your own thing" and "whatever turns you on" come to the surface as indicative of the affect of Zen Buddhism on traditional Western thought. These phrases are reflective of Zen influence on relativism, i.e., the idea that all religions are about the same or of almost equal value. The current emphasis on celebration of the presence of Christ has been learned from Zen because Zen emphasizes an awareness of his vital experiences.

Astrology is an ancient Eastern alternate to religion which has become vastly popular in the United States in the past decade. Today more than 72 percent of the 1750 daily newspapers in the United States carry horoscope columns with forty million daily readers. Astrology is currently a $200-million annual business in the United States. Daily more than a thousand computerized horoscopes are turned out by one single company in New York City. There are currently more than fifteen thousand full-time and 175,000 part-time astrologers in the United States. For many, astrology has replaced psychology as the unraveller of this age's behavior. Contemporary "priest-astrologers" in America use techniques which would be readily understood by Babylonian magi millenia ago and by Chinese astrologers even further back in time.

Hinduism has had its effect on American religious thought. The Gallup Poll on Religion issued in 1969 showed that twenty percent of the adult citizens of the United States now believe in reincarnation. Nonviolence as a method of social change was learned from a Hindu prophet named Mahatma Gandhi.

America's youth are busy learning about religions which were formerly considered part of another world—a world of pagodas, camels, elephants, and monks with shaved heads. This author surveyed two hundred seventh- and eighth-grade students at a Baptist assembly.

In response to an inquiry as to whether they had written a term paper on an Eastern religion as part of a school assignment, more than half of the students replied in the affirmative. The world is shrinking, especially in the area of religious awareness.

East has not only met, but considerably affected the concept of religion held in the Western world.

American Buddhism

Wind Bell is a quarterly publication of the Zen Center in San Francisco. A recent issue contains a lecture by a resident Zen teacher at the retreat center near Tassajara, California.

Shunryu Suzuki Roshi said: "Before you attain enlightenment, enlightenment is there. It is not because one attains
enlightenment that enlightenment is there. Enlightenment is
always there and if you realize this, that is enlightenment."[1]

These words sound as foreign as they really are to most
Christians of the Western world. They will, however, sound
less foreign by the year 1980 because Buddhism is becoming better known and more widely accepted in the United
States. Buddhists in the fifty states now number more than
three hundred thousand. Already there are more Buddhists
in America than in India, the land of this religion's birth.

As an organized movement, Buddhism came to America
in 1896 when two Japanese priests arrived in San Francisco
to establish congregations. In 1905 the first Buddhist temple
was consecrated there. Evidences of acclimation to American culture are prevalent, such as Christmas with candy
and Santa Claus and a graded Sunday School program.
However, presently most Buddhists in America are of Orien-
tal background. As the movement grows, there will be more
public witnessing to their faith in terms evangelical Christians can understand. Most Buddhist leaders are aware of
their becoming Americanized and are reflecting upon it in
their periodicals. The following excerpts from an article in
The American Buddhist is but one example of this identity
crisis:

. . . Much of our present Buddhist practices can be understood
and appreciated only by those who are familiar with the customs
and thoughts associated with Japan. On the other hand, our present Buddhism in America is American Buddhism in that many of
our present practices and philosophy of church administration and
leadership have been revised in its interpretation and function so
as to suit the total sociological climate of this country.[2]

Gautama Buddha, who lived in the sixth century B.C.,
was primarily concerned with the pain and meaninglessness

of human life and sought to provide a channel into a realm of nonbeing where there is no time, pain, or death. The goal is Nirvana, the complete opposite of pain or anxiety. It is the deathless state encompassing the end of all suffering and frustration, a free state of mind. According to most sects of modern Buddhism in America, this state can be reached in one's earthly existence. Parinirvana is a higher state which can be reached only after one dies. For the Buddhist, this is the ultimate or the eternal state.

Students of Buddhist doctrine disagree as to whether it teaches atheism. Buddhism can be called atheistic because it denies the existence of a Creator or any being who stands outside of man and the world or of any power that judges the action of man. However, Buddha's followers do recognize the law of Karma, the idea that one's deliberately willed actions produce future mental and physical results in keeping with their original quality. As one can see, Buddhists are only atheistic in the denial of an ultimate personal being called God. They live with many of the same principles and attributes which Christians do, yet in an impersonal manner.

The fundamental differences in Buddhist teaching and evangelical Christian doctrine are evident:

1. Buddhism emphasizes the impersonal law of karma; Christians the personal Law-Giver.
2. Nonexistence is the ideal goal for the Buddhist, whereas Christians believe that human life is the gift of God and is designed to have existence forever.
3. Nirvana is salvation from life, while the Christian's entry into the kingdom of God denotes new birth into a life of joy and love.
4. The way of salvation is different in that the individual is far more dependent on himself in Buddhism than is the Christian with his emphasis on God's grace.

So, on what evanglical Christians consider to be the fundamental questions of religion and human existence, the two faith systems are widely divergent.

Despite these differences, Buddhism continues to grow in the United States. American Buddhism is primarily that of the Mahayana tradition. Mahayana Buddhism arose in northwest India between the third century before Christ. Adherents of this liberal sect have respect for the *bodhisattva,* a person so in sympathy with the sufferings of all human beings that he refuses to enter into Nirvana until all others can enter with him.

The most outstanding bodhisattva for most mahayanists is Amida Buddha, who is esteemed next to Gautama, the original Buddha. They believe that anyone who has faith in Amida will at death enter into the "Pure Land," a western paradise. Another bodhisattva is Kwan-Yin, the goddess of mercy who took a vow to help anyone who needs her.

The three major Buddhist groups in America follow the three main divisions in Mahayana Buddhism found in Japan and Korea: the "Pure Land" whose central doctrine is faith in Amida; the "Intuitive," the primary example being Zen; and the "socio-political," characterized by Sokagakkai.

The American Buddhist Association was founded in 1959 to study and propagate Amida Buddhism. It is only one of many similar groups.

Zen is a form of intuitive Buddhism which often cuts across lives of religious preference. The central teaching is the principle of allowing the mind to operate freely.

Zen in America has been popularized through the works of D. T. Suzuki, author of the three-volume work, *Essays in Zen Buddhism,*[3] as well as more than twenty other books on the subject. His writing skill helps to account for the popularity of Zen in the academic community.

Zen's freedom from patterned thinking affords many persons a mental frame of reference for rebellion against what they consider society's rigid thought forms. It is popular among the youth subculture because it allows new patterns for thought.

One's life and thinking changes in Zen with the experience of satori, or enlightenment. A description of the moment of satori reveals its nature as an awakening:

Ztt! I entered. I lost the boundary of my physical body. I had my skin, of course, but I felt I was standing in the center of the cosmos. . . . I had never known this world before. I had believed that I was created, but now I must change my opinion: I was never created; I was created, but now I must change my opinion. I was never created; I was the cosmos; no individual . . . existed.[4]

The most militant and flourishing company of Buddhists in the United States are the members of Soka Gakkai, a lay organization. There are 34,000 members of the organization in the United States. It publishes the *World Tribune,* a weekly newspaper. Members of the group are frequently exhorted to missionary activity, because they believe that the Japanese are an advanced people with the true religion. Individual effort is given much emphasis, and individual members are advanced in the organization according to their activity on behalf of the group.

Buddhism will lose the "foreign" look as it gains popularity in America. The Witnessing Christian can counter Buddhist growth by emphasizing the finality of Christ and the value of personal relationships. An evangelical Christian's friendship and testimony to the happiness found in Christ is an indictment against the Buddhist claim that religious faith is impersonal.

American Hindus

The oldest of the world's religions claims the allegiance of 80 percent of the more than 450 million people in India.

Hinduism permeates life in the nation of India and is beginning to do so in the United States. Estimates of the number of Hindus in our nation ranges from 150,000 to 200,000 or about one tenth of 1 percent of the population.

A definition for Hinduism is difficult to formulate, for as a religion it embodies much ancient folklore of India, customs of the people, social caste distinctions, and modern reform movements such as Vedanta. However, it is valid to speak of Hinduism as a somewhat unified religion because most Hindus do share common scriptures, deities, ideals, beliefs, and worship practices. Fairly specialized forms of this world religion are prevalent in the United States, which makes the wake of classical Hinduism easier to decipher on the American scene.

Most modern Hindus hold in common several major areas of belief. The first of these is the doctrine of karma, which decrees that every responsible decision must have its determinate consequences. Another common doctrine held by most modern Hindus is their idea of the composition of man. This begins with the atman or "inner self," which remains as the individual's permanent and unchanging substance. Man is held by the Hindu to be a layered being, composed of a body and of a conscious and subconscious personality. In order to be a "real" person, one is to "know" himself but not confuse his real self (atman) with his outward self.

Perhaps the most popularized idea in Hinduism is reincarnation. Most Hindus see as the most desirable outcome of death his absorption into Brahman or an escape from the cycle of reincarnation. This absorption, however, seldom occurs and the person is supposedly reborn into some form of animal, vegetable, or insect life. The kind of life into which the person is reborn depends on his responsibility in his prior life to the law of karma. Hinduism views the world as going through cycle after cycle in time, being governed by karma, being deceptive in trying to pass itself off as ultimate reality, and primarily as a training ground for advancement toward their concept of God.

The Hindu thinks that what man needs is deliverance (moksha) from the endless cycle of reincarnation governed by karma and the limitations of individual existence. There is little concept of man's sinfulness. Hinduism teaches that the enslaved man is held by his own actions and condemned to be reborn.

Escape from this fate can come in one of three ways to the Hindu: through works (karma yoga) such as showing hospitality to one's neighbor; through knowledge (Jnana Yoga) by deep meditation, or through devotion (Bhakti Yoga) by worshiping God. All of these efforts come under the broader heading of yoga, which is the term for working out one's escape from his limited life. So, life itself is not what each person is reaching for, but he desires instead escape from life to a higher level of existence. The message of Hinduism seems to be something like this: live out your life doing what you know to be right, so that finally you may enter into eternal peace through deliverance from the limitations of your present life.

The first Hindu sect in the United States was formed in 1894 by Swami Vivekananda, a follower of Ramakrishna. The Vedanta Society works in conjunction with the Ramakrishna Mission which has more than 160 centers of propagation in a dozen countries. Vedantists feel a strong compulsion to spread their faith all over the world. Vivekananda himself wrote, "This is the great ideal before us . . . the conquest of the whole world by India . . . and we must get ready for it . . . up, India, and conquer the world with your spirituality."[5]

Vedanta philosophy consists of three propositions: man

is really divine, the aim of life is to recognize this divine
nature, and all religions are essentially in agreement. Vivekananda said: "If there is ever to be a universal religion,
it must be one which will have no location in place or time;
which will be infinite, like the God it will preach, and whose
sun will shine upon the followers of Krishna and of Christ."[6]
Vedanta is so capable of assimilation that it sees no diffi-
culty in accepting Christ as *a* son of God.

In most cases, Vedanta appeals to seekers of truth who
have no definite religious tradition, so Hinduism becomes
their first vital religion. This mission-oriented philosophy has
made such inroads into the American religious scene that it
is regarded by some evangelical Christians as the greatest
danger to Christianity in our nation today.[7]

Gurus have appealed to thousands in the United States
over the past decades, offering certain forms of Hinduism
as alternatives to Christian discipleship. The best-known
among evangelical Christians is probably Maharishi Mahesh
Yogi, because of the publicity given him through the mass
media. The Beatles and Mia Farrow state that Maharishi
changed their lives. Heralded as the new prophet of peace
and individual serenity, he preaches a method of knowing
oneself called "transcendental meditation." Maharishi says,
"Anyone can do it. Because anyone who can think, and
through thought bring his awareness outward, can reverse
the process of thinking and take the awareness to a source
of thought."[8] The guru maintains that what he is saying is
not a unique new religion, but only a method of finding
peace. However, it should be noted that the presuppositions of Maharishi's are Hindu in origin. This is clear in
the following quote, "The basis of my meditation is the desire of mind to go to a field of greater happiness, the innate
tendency of the mind to go to a field of greater happiness;
and the being is of blissful nature."[9]

The Hindu concept of the mind seeking absorption into bliss is a preconceived notion which the guru brings to his method. Jesus, on the other hand, talked more of involvement in bringing the kingdom of God to earth. Maharishi Mahesh Yogi is but one among hundreds of resident gurus who have found fertile soil of acceptance in the changing American religious climate.

The Hare Krishna Movement has confronted many dwellers of modern cities by street chanting and the passing out of tracts and sale of books. Hare Krishna chanters follow Swami A. C. Bhaktivedanta, who founded the International Society for Krishna Consciousness in 1966. They claim that by the continual chanting of the Hindu names for God, one can find the sublime life. The oft-repeated chant is as follows:

> HARE KRISHNA HARE KRISHNA
> KRISHNA KRISHNA HARE HARE
> IIARE RAMA HARE RAMA
> RAMA RAMA HARE HARE

Roughly translated, the chant means "Oh, the Glories of the Lord, Oh, His Energies."

Swami A. C. Bhaktivedanta traces his disciplic succession all the way back to a time five thousand years ago when the Lord Krishna (an appearance of God) spoke the *Bhagavad-gita*, a famous piece of Hindu literature.

The Hare Krishna chanters ascribe to Krishna many of the same characteristics Christians do to Christ. This is obvious in the following statement: "Lord Sri Krsna is the Absolute Truth, the Supreme Personality of Godhead. . . . He has a body made of eternity, bliss and all knowledge. God has infinite forms and expansions."[10]

The International Society for Krishna Consciousness is a fast-growing aspect of Hindu-type movements in America. It continues to appeal to many college students who are interested in new ways of seeking God. Evangelical Christians, especially in major metropolitan areas, will be faced with the question of witnessing to the Hare Krishna chanters.

Tolerance and the Christ

The influx of the Eastern religions into the Western world has caused several divergent reactions to this invasion. Some would over-react and maintain that the Eastern religions should be kept from proselyting from among western, and especially, evangelical Christians. E. Luther Copeland, a Baptist professor, speaks of missions, thoughtfully to this point:

> We believe in religious freedom even for those who deny our faith and try to convert us to some other religion. . . . Christian tolerance is not based on agnosticism the idea that we really cannot know ultimate or final truth. Nor is it based on relativism, the notion that all religions are primarily cultural products, and that therefore none of them can claim any final revelation. . . . The Christian's tolerance is that of one who believes that God has spoken a final word to all mankind in Jesus Christ.[11]

Kenneth Cragg points out that the revolutionary impact of Christ can be trusted to take care of itself in the open market of free discussion. Therefore, he urges the Christian to learn to hold "positive premises without negative inferences.[12] By this he means that the Christian can hold to the truth he knows in Christ without being highly judgmental about or denying religious freedom to the one who disagrees with him.

Christ is the standard by which all religions are to be judged. He is the final or ultimate, revelation of God. Dow Kirkpatrick points out five ways in which Christ is final:

1. To know Jesus Christ is to know God in a way not available in any other revelation.

2. What is available to be known in Jesus is all that man needs to know about God.
3. The whole event of Jesus Christ defines essential human nature.
4. The above claims are not only made valid, but made available to all men by the unique aliveness of Jesus Christ in man's experience.
5. Man's history is finally judged by its approximation to the nature of God whose nature is revealed in Jesus Christ.[13]

Tolerance in Christ is based on the love shown by him, not on ignorance of him. Personal experience with Christ enables one to know him in a way which compels him to love others, even of vastly different world perspectives.

How to Witness

This author has discovered in dozens of witnessing sessions with members of Eastern religions that the following guidelines are applicable:

1. Avoid polemic which makes little of the religion or religious commitment of the communicant.
2. Avoid being placed in a position of defending Western culture or Christianity as producer of a justice-oriented society.
3. Present the totality of the unique and miraculous Christ-event, including the incarnation of the Son of God, his teachings, leadership ability, sin-free life, sacrificial death, and significant and unduplicated resurrection.
4. Stress individual commitment and personal reliance on Christ. Many world religionists believe in an impersonal God and that all religions are of almost equal merit.
5. Recognize truths to be found in other religious traditions. Stress that God has revealed himself most clearly in Jesus of Nazareth.
6. Stress the heavenly Father as a loving God (see John 1:1–18).

7. Emphasize clear communication (use of modern new translations will be of great value, e.g., *Good News for Modern Man*).

Patience, prayer, and genuine interest in persons are important in implementing these guidelines. Eastern religions are forcing Christians to be more serious about direct experience of the unique Christ. Christianity can survive the onslaught of Eastern values only if Christ is followed truly.

Chapter VII

UNITARIAN-UNIVERSALISTS: ONE GOD, AT THE MOST

Affirmation of God's unity is the fundamental premise of Unitarianism, as the name implies. Most evangelical Christians are avowed trinitarians, i.e., believers in the Trinity as it expresses God being Father, Son, and Holy Spirit. Some hypercritical observers of the Unitarian faith have characterized these adherents as believing in "one God, at the most." This criticism is often aimed thoughtlessly at the Unitarians without a study of what they mean to say when affirming the unity of God. Giving reason the central place in religious experience, Unitarians have a long history of seeking to work out a logical faith system.

Forty years before John Adams was to become the second president of the United States, he recorded in his diary that he was giving up his thoughts of becoming a minister. He wrote, "I saw a spirit of dogmatism and bigotry in clergy and laity, that, if I should be a priest, I must take my side, and pronounce as positively as any of them, or never get a parish, or getting it must soon leave it." He then resolved that he was not made for the pulpit in such times, since such a life promised only "endless altercations" with little chance of doing good to his fellowmen! Adams was expressing the constant dilemma of the freethinker in religious matters, i.e., to what extent search for doctrinal truth interferes with social righteousness. This dilemma is still present to some who seek discipleship.

Two hundred thousand persons in the United States have

chosen to solve the problem by saying that creeds and doctrinal statements do not matter since they are simply a reflection of selected religious thought at a specific time. These persons are members of the Unitarian Universalist Association, which was consolidated in May of 1961. They stand in impressive company. Besides John Adams, four other presidents have been Unitarians: Jefferson, John Quincy Adams, Fillmore, and Taft. American literary figures who were part of this sentiment include Emerson, Thoreau, Hawthorne, Longfellow, and Lowell. Other reformers and innovators include Susan B. Anthony, Horace Mann, and Samuel Morse.

Brief History

Unitarianism gained notoriety in the Western world when Michael Servetus (1511-1553) wrote a book entitled *On the Errors of the Trinity* in 1531. He was burned at the stake by followers of John Calvin in Geneva. A strong Unitarian movement developed in Poland under the leadership of Faustus Socinus (1539-1604), a strong propogator of anti-Trinitarian doctrines. Francis David led the movement in Hungary, came under close scrutiny by the church, and died in prison in 1579. He contended that Jesus was not God and should not be worshiped as Deity. David's followers were the first to be taunted by the satirical word, "Unitarians."

The founder of the Unitarian Church in England was Theophilus Lindsey, who conducted a service in 1774 before a large London congregation, including Benjamin Franklin and one Joseph Priestly. Twenty years later Priestly gathered a congregation together in Northumberland, Pennsylvania, the first on American soil to call itself Unitarian.

The Unitarians fought the Calvinists of the late eighteenth and early nineteenth century on several points, including the deity of Christ, predestination, human depravity, and hell fire.

The religious-thought world of the first half of the nineteenth century was shocked into the realization that Unitarian thought was becoming more influential, as word spread about three addresses given by three outstanding pulpiteers. The place was Baltimore and the year was 1819 when William Ellery Channing stood to preach the ordination sermon of a young minister. Channing's open-minded approach to religious problems had led him to help found a magazine, *The Christian Disciple*, the voice of the Boston Liberals. In his Baltimore sermon, Channing said, "Revelation is addressed to us as a rational being. . . . We believe, then, that Christ is one mind, one being, and I add, a being distinct from the one God. . . . "[1] The stage was set for turmoil within Congregationalism.

Ralph Waldo Emerson had Channing for his pastor as a young man at Harvard College where Channing helped mold his religious thought patterns. When Emerson addressed the Divinity School there in 1838, he opened the ears of his hearers with such pronouncements as:

He [Jesus Christ] spoke of miracles; for he felt that man's life was a miracle. . . . But the word miracle, as pronounced by Christian churches, gives a false impression; it is monster. . . . The Hebrew and Greek Scriptures contain immortal sentences, . . . But they have no epical integrity; are fragmentary; are not shown in their order to the intellect.[2]

Theodore Parker, another minister, heard Emerson deliver his address at the Harvard Divinity School and was duly impressed. Three years later Parker himself made explicit his Unitarian views in an address given in Boston which he entitled, "The Transient and Permanent in Christianity." His listeners heard such words as:

Anyone who traces the history of what is called Christianity, will see that nothing changes more from day to day than the doctrines taught as Christian, and insisted on as essential to Christianity and personal salvation. What is falsehood in one province passes for truth in another.[3]

Parker went on to write *Discourses of Matters Pertaining to Religion* which was accused of being vehemently heretical, but the die was cast. By then the Unitarians were very much in evidence 'on the religious scene in America and never to be removed therefrom. In the meantime the American Unitarian Association had been formed in 1825. A national conference was established in 1865. In the 1884 meeting of this national conference the nature of the American Unitarian Association was changed from a loose association of individual believers to an organization of churches.

The movement called Universalism ran a separate course until 1961, when the Unitarian Universalist Association was formed. John Murray, an English Universalist, came to New Jersey in 1770. He had been influenced by the writings of James Relly, an advocate of universal salvation. Murray became minister of the first organized church in America in 1779 in Gloucester, Massachusetts. He told his parishioners, "Give the people, not Hell, but hope and courage. Do not push them deeper into their theological despair, but preach the kindness and everlasting love of God." In 1786, the Universalist Baptist Church was formed in Philadelphia, under the leadership of Elhanan Ulinchester, who had come to his Universalist views independently of Murray.

The primary theologian of the Universalist movement was Hosea Ballou, who wrote *Treatise on Atonement* in 1805, renouncing the doctrines of the deprivity of the human race and everlasting punishment.

By 1894, the Universalists had grown to sufficient size to form "The Universalist General Convention" and four years later appointed Isaac M. Atwood as first general superintendent. In 1899 the General Convention met in Boston and adopted the "Essential Principles of the Universalist Church," including the tenet for the final harmony of all souls with God.

The high point in twentieth-century Universalism came in 1961 with the merger with Unitarians. The new organization was possible because of the common beliefs the two groups already held, including the supreme worth of every human personality and a free search for truth. The movement of Unitarian-Universalism has now grown to include more than seven hundred churches and four hundred and fifty fellowships. Church school enrolment and adult membership now approaches two hundred thousand in the United States.

Basic Beliefs

All Unitarian-Universalist doctrines rest on the principle of the free mind and the role of reason in the search for religious truth. One corollary to the use of the free mind in religion is the distrust of creeds. In other words, "Freedom of belief in matters of religion means that nothing which has been handed down from the past is acceptable as a complete and final exposition of all truth."[4] Because of this, it is difficult to pinpoint the beliefs of this movement, but certain themes keep recurring.

On the matter of salvation, Channing set the stage in 1821 when he said, "Our proper work is to approach God by the free and natural unfolding of our highest powers."[5] Man is not seen to be a fallen sinner in need of miraculous salvation but as a being worthy and capable of bringing about his own salvation through work for love, justice and freedom. Since man is not condemned by original sin, he is capable of "self-improvement."

George Marshall continues this train of thought in a recent pamphlet: "We believe in salvation by character, that is, man is capable of achieving a more ideal life by the results of his own efforts to strengthen and sensitize himself. We do not rely on some supernatural intervention."[6]

Unitarians regard the Bible as a piece of great literature while subjecting it critically to the rule of reason. Mr. Marshall phrases it as follows:

We find it [the Bible] to offer great lessons, fine poetry, important records, understood best with archeological aid and comparison with other cultures and literature. We also find that it contains much unimportant material. Unitarians and Universalists use their reason when they study the Bible, and it becomes a larger Bible in consequence.[7]

An evangelical Christian may wonder whether the Bible becomes "larger" the way Unitarians view it.

As mentioned earlier, Unitarians have taken their name because of their view of the oneness of God. Channing spoke for most Unitarians when he said, in 1819, "We object to the doctrine of the Trinity, that, while acknowledging in words, it subverts in effect, the unity of God."[8] The key word here is "unity," and most Unitarians believe that classical Christian statements of the Trinity tend to do injustice to the uni-personality of God.

A corollary of this stance, however, is that the Holy Spirit is identified with the Father himself, being a holy influence rather than a person. Jesus is revered as a great teacher and the best among men. One Unitarian writer comes to the conclusion that "The Jesus portrayed in the Gospels is a confusing and bewildering figure. It is pertinent to honor Buddha, Zoroaster, Isaiah, and Confucius, no less than Jesus for symbolizing compassion, unselfishness, self-sacrifice and good will."[9] According to most of these believers, the primary reason that Jesus came to earth was to be a moral example. They affirm the normal humanity of Jesus and not the eternal deity of Christ.

Universalists have contributed to this association the idea

that eventually all men will be saved; or, if any soul is saved, none is ultimately lost. S. H. Mellone wrote, "Final communion with God is the destiny of every soul, and not alone those who know in this present by living experience what such communion is."[10] This concept has given a large popular appeal for Unitarianism to those in America with relativistic tendencies in comparative religion.

Man is said to be basically good and the child of God, standing high on the evolutionary ladder with great potential for growth. Human nature in the present tense does not separate man from God but binds him together with God. Jesus Christ supposedly not only taught that he was divine but also that all men are divine. It follows, then, that man is to find religious meaning and truth by right use of the powers God gives him.

Unitarian-Universalists have no creed, but the aforementioned views of God, man and the world do permeate the thought world of most members of this association. Subscription to a formal creed is not necessary for a people to be creedal, however, as Unitarians and all those in the free church tradition know quite well.

What They Can Teach Us

Unitarian-Universalists can teach tradition-oriented Christians a great deal. For one thing, "All Unitarians would agree that the impact of religion on individual human society must be ethical—or it would be worthless."[11] Unitarians have continually stressed the practical application of religious faith. This emphasis has produced important leadership, including Dorothy Dix in woman's suffrage and George W. Quimby, leader of opposition to capital punishment. Unitarians have realized that social problems demand social action and have therefore organized to meet social needs. Since 1908, they have had the Unitarian Fellowship for Social Justice with the stated purpose of "the realization of religious ideals in present day society."[12] Evangelical Christians would do well to allow the Spirit of Christ to permeate the courthouse lest he perish on the modern-day steeple. Close attention should be paid to those advocating that the gospel is potentially redemptive in every area of life, individual and social.

Distrust or misuse of reason within the religious experience by evangelical Christians has been a deterrent to reaching basically intellectual persons with the gospel. Unitarians have appealed to this same group with a strong emphasis on the free search for truth—religious, scientific or moral—wherever it is to be found. The constitution of the Unitarian Universalist Association lists as its first aim, "To strengthen one another in a free and disciplined search for truth as the foundation of our religious fellowship."[13] This means the admission that there may be religious truth in Buddhism, scientific truth in some theories of evolution, and moral truth in Judaism. By coupling the responsible use of reason with the spiritual truths in the living and written Word, evangelical Christians may learn that God's truth is not confined in specific creeds, denomination or movements.

A third lesson traditional Christians would do well to learn from Unitarians is the development of a spirit of toleration. Burning at the stake stands as a symbol of the Unitarians' struggle against persecution. This struggle coupled with disdain for creeds and doctrinal certainty has given the movement an overarching appreciation for the differences and common aspirations of all peoples. Some Christians have assumed that "cornering" the truth of God has given them the right to degrade the beliefs of others. Christians can learn to hold to truth while granting others the liberty to find truth for themselves. This can serve as a reminder that the granting of religious liberty does not necessitate theological relativism, but always does demand the recognition of the dignity of the believer. The tendency toward sectarian attitude in comparative religion, i.e., the idea that one's convictions are correct and others are the incorrect assumptions of a deluded people, can be avoided by the granting of full religious liberty. This is the spirit of religious toleration granted by Unitarian-Universalists, a spirit to be emulated.

Evangelical Christianity loses constantly some of its brightest followers because of the attraction of free thought and social relevance. When this is recognized and dealt with, this loss can radically wane.

Critical Analysis

Representing the liberal wing of Christianity, Unitarian-Universalism does have certain weaknesses when viewed from the dual standard of Scripture and the risen Lord.

There is a question as to whether Unitarianism can be called Christian. When asked this question directly, one of their leaders replied:

If Christianity means a respect and reverence for Jesus and what He sought to be and do in His own time; if Christianity means the effort to bring to birth in our lives today something of 'that Spirit which was in Jesus'—then Unitarians have as good a right as anybody else to call themselves Christian.[14]

This quote makes it clear that Unitarianism defines Christianity as emulation of the spirit and teachings of Jesus, with little attention given to his divine nature. Lacking is the affirmation of the total Christ-event including the virgin birth, miracle of the incarnation, his death, and glorious resurrection.

The high place Unitarians have given reason in determining religious truth has tended to bring about such statements as, "The substance of religion is to nurture reason." The recognition of the proper use of reason in religious faith and practice is one matter, but to allow it to preempt the regenerate spiritual and emotional growth of the Christian is another. The basic question in comparative religion, of course, is that of the source of authority. The Christian need not forget his mind as he searches for God's truth in the scripture and the world, but on the other hand, he need not eliminate the possibility of miracle in the name of reason. Elton Trueblood sheds valuable light on this question when he writes:

Since the supposition that we must choose between clearmindedness and reverence is something that has no foundation in fact, the rational evangelical is the new man for our generation. It is the vocation of the Christian intellectual to be both tough-minded and tender-hearted, and to be both at once.[15]

Because of the prominent role given to reason by the Unitarians, their view of the Holy Scripture is greatly affected. Many Unitarians believe that the Bible is a record of the events of history in the remote past. "The natural character of the Bible" is upheld as opposed to the view that God has revealed uniquely in this written Word his will for every generation. To affirm that God used and still uses human instruments to record and do his will is different than asserting that the Bible is unique, especially in light of its witness to the Son.

Unitarian-Universalists disagree with one emphasis of the Hebrew-Christian faith, i.e., the sinful nature of man. The corollary to this view is that final communion with God is the destiny of every soul. Heaven and hell are held to be meaningful only for names and conditions within the human spirit. Man is seen to be potentially good and capable of perfectability. No need is seen for the atoning death of Christ. This is to ignore the teachings of both the Old and New Testaments that "Whosoever hath sinned against me, him will I blot out of my book" (Ex. 32:33*b*) and "Behold the Lamb of God, which taketh away the sin of the World" (John 1:29*b*). To assert that man does not stand in need of salvation is also to ignore men such as Hitler and deeds such as murder, rape, greed, and war. For guilt-ridden modern man, it is to fail to provide a release for this guilt. To contend for the dignity of man is not to say that man's worth has not been raised by self-appropriated grace and glorious resurrected presence of Christ through the Holy Spirit.

The issue remains, as phrased by Earl Morse Wilbur, "A conflict between the claims of perfectly free inquiry on the one hand and the limitations of supernatural revelation on the other."[16] The Christian thinker, following the pattern of Christ who astounded the rabbis with his knowledge, should balance faith with reason. "Free inquiry" ideally includes the liberating influence of supernatural revelation. To ignore light given by special revelation is to block out a vast storehouse of knowledge and to block free inquiry in the search for truth.

To view Jesus as merely another prophet after one has met him as Lord is an experiential impossibility. Yet, Unitarian-Universalist congregations are filled with former evangelical Christians who grew tired of churches where dogmatic rigidity replaced an open-ended experience with Christ.

Evangelical Christians must take notice, or watch those persons who could make the best contributions to the Kingdom continue to leave in search of freedom.

Conclusion

CULTIVATING THE CULTISTS

Regardless of the label—cults, sects, deviations, or alternatives—the groups under discussion in this book grow because they minister to persons. Those persons may be isolated individuals seeking love or emotionally disturbed persons in search of healing. Group identity and purpose in zeal give these persons the direction they seek. Evangelical Christians can minister best in this wage of pluralism by copying the strong points of those groups with which they hope to serve. For example, Christian Scientists may often be reached by showing authentic concern for the areas in their life which need healing. This may be called cultivation evangelism, i.e., acting in Christian love toward the total needs of a fellow human until such time as the verbal proclamation of God's love in Christ flows from one loving and trusting heart to another.

If C. W. Brister is correct in defining the church as, "a community of Christians who care for one another and seek by varied means to extend that care to persons outside the church,"[1] the care will be a contagious part of the church.

Typical of some of the alternative groups' attitude toward those within "Christendom" is the Jehovah's Witness assertion that clergymen are "an unselfish class . . . afar off from God and dead to his favor."[2] Often American evangelical Christians have returned the compliment, being more than glad to slam the front door in the face of a pair of Latter-Day Saint missionaries or a Jehovah's Witness considered to be pests or impossible persons with which to communicate. However, to shut out a person who has come to discuss religious matters is to pass up a ready-made opportunity for witness. To doubt that communication of spiritual truth may take place under such circumstances is to display a lack of faith in the convincing power of the Holy Spirit.

The recommended guidelines for such an occasion are as follows:

1. Befriend them and listen attentively to their beliefs. Many cultists urgently seek acceptance, a need which prompted them to join their group in the first place.
2. Rely finally on the Holy Spirit to convict.
3. Speak not only of the sinfulness of man but of the positive and loving attributes of God. In the teachings of many alternative groups, God is thought to be "as terrible as an army with banners of wrath." Love, joy, peace, and purpose in living for Christ should be stressed.
4. Realize that the matter of authority often may have to be discussed before fruitful dialogue may occur. God has revealed himself uniquely in the written and living Word because these instruments show most clearly his love and watchcare. Evangelical Christians maintain that the Holy Spirit continues to reveal through the Word and will give no revelation contrary to it. The member of the alternate group should be confronted with the puzzling question of why God seemingly contradicts himself in their later revelations.
5. Recognize that cultists often redefine biblical terms. They do not mean the same by grace, faith, resurrection, gospel, and other terms that evangelicals do.
6. Avoid condemnation and castigation of the cultist as a person. Avoid also any indication that evangelical Christians

consider him deranged, ignorant or uncommitted. Your offensive is against his theology, not his person. Beware of the temptation to win an argument and lose opportunity for further witnessing.

7. Stress the totality and uniqueness of the Christ-event. Evangelical Christians often move too frequently to the atoning death of Jesus, overlooking other redemptive aspects of his life.

Maintenance of personal piety through Bible study and prayer is important to the potential witness to the cultist. However, this is only part of the total picture of individual and collective sanctification which the witness should be constantly cultivating. In the midst of expanding pluralism, evangelical churches can hardly afford the luxury of delinquent converts. The retarded convert can be led to growth when several common assumptions among evangelicals are eradicated.

One area of neglect is the false separation between the "secular" and the "religious" in the living out of the gospel. If conversion is seen merely as a distinctly "religious" happening, the implication is that the event occurs in isolation from the world outside. Christian growth tends to be measured in "religious" categories and it becomes possible to despise or be apathetic toward other persons in God's creation.

Piety often fails to produce because it is seen as directed solely toward the end of personal purity. Purity should not be seen as an end in itself but as a tool for witness in all areas of life—social, personal, and political.

Today evangelical churches are faced with an identity crisis, partially due to the rise of alternatives to discipleship. Langdon Gilkey spoke to one aspect of the problem:

The word that is heard in the church is often either an irrelevant, unrelated "gospel" that heals no one because it sears no one, or merely the accepted wisdom of the world, untransformed by any transcendent judging and healing elements, and therefore also ultimately sterile.[3]

Christian growth is evident in the fact that the maturing Christian progressively sees his role in judgment of earthly society. Therefore, his actions and pronouncements are not sterile, but life-giving. This can occur when evangelical churches decide that they are neither second-rate social clubs nor havens for those who seek reinforcement of prejudice or injustice. When the church's unique identity is closely linked with sanctification, it becomes the living out of Christ's demands in all of life with attention given to the value of man.

Another area in which improvement can be shown is in what William Hordern calls "the theologianhood of all believers."[4] Intellectual growth is too often viewed with suspicion rather than seen as part of sanctification. Interchange of ideas on the Christian faith is often equated with compromise. If communication across religious lines is to occur, openness is necessary. The believer who wears another denominational or religious tag has a lot to contribute to an understanding of God and Christ. A related problem is that theology is seen as a specialized business of the expert rather than the legitimate business of the layman. Especially in the area of witnessing across religious lines, the layman is better equipped by virtue of his daily vocation to explain his faith in the language of the world. Yet, the layman has been denied his theological birthright, and, as a result, listens and reads language from pulpit and religious literature which he can barely comprehend and relate.

Sanctification or commitment of the total person to Christ is necessary to witness in an age peopled with alternatives. Conversion and Christian growth is concerned with more than the soul. The cults grow because of their ministry to other aspects of the personality. As a corrective, evangelicals might take the definition of Christian growth offered by Emil Brunner:

God wins back for Himself, step by step, starting from the personal center, the heart, which has heard the word of justification, pressing forward into the surrounding territories toward the periphery, by taking control of the various sections of human feeling, thought and will, and even reshaping his unconscious self.[5]

Dr. Brunner speaks directly to the issue of offering the world the good news of Christ, not a set of rules. Many in the alternative groups await a positive note of release coupled with demonstrative love from evangelical Christians. He writes:

A sanctification which is cut adrift from faith in Christ can be nothing but moralism. This moralism is constituted by an inability to break free from the law, from general rules of obligation. . . . This legalism is to blame for the lack of imagination in average Christianity, which ever and again sacrifices the spontaneity of love to legalistic rule-of-thumb and leaves in practice hardly any room for the embodiment of the creative, intuitive and unpharasaic freedom of God's children. People have not dared really to live in the Spirit.[6]

The gospel which evangelical Christians offer to the world is the good news that God is love and sets one free. This is the positive note in freedom which evangelicals offer.

The offer of this good news can come naturally by the development of dialogue. If what the alternative groups have is truth, it will stand in open debate. The same is true for evangelical Christians. Dialogue on an individual or group basis could aid evangelical Christians in several areas. They include:

1. Reformation through redefining essential faith patterns;
2. Rediscovery of forgotten truths;
3. Discovery of the gospel's relevance to the whole man;
4. New light on common problems among evangelicals and cultists;
5. Development of a workable method of Bible interpretation;

6. Appreciation for the positive role of the alternative groups;

7. Renewed awareness of the finality of Christ.

This open dialogue can create a spirit of ministry to each other. This can avoid the type of isolated denominationalism which H. Richard Niebuhr warned against more than four decades ago:

> The evil of denominationalism lies in the conditions which fashion them into caste-organizations, to sublimate their loyalties to standards and institutions only remotely relevant if not contrary to the Christian ideal, to resist the temptation of making their own self-preservation and extension the primary object of their endeavor.[7]

The more frequent the contact between evangelicals and cultists, the more likely to develop the intensity of experience which once more accurately described evangelicals.

Dialogue on doctrinal differences can be helpful in calling evangelicals back to forgotten truths. The recognition will come that not all being taught by cultists is error. For example, Jehovah's Witnesses have long taught that the soul is a principle of life, not an entity. Their interpretation of Genesis 2:7 correctly sees the Hebrew word *nephesh* as carrying the idea of life, not "soul." Extensive discussion between evangelicals and Jehovah's Witnesses can help to erase the body-soul dichotomy in the minds of Baptist laymen. This will serve as a balance to the Witnesses' doctrine that man is mortal. Truth will emerge in open and frank dialogue as both groups are called to reformation.

Continual dialogue can throw new light on common problems among evangelicals and the cults. A most obvious issue is that of the role of the Negro in the Christian community. This is a perpetual problem to the Mormons, who deny the right of the Melchizedek priesthood to Negroes. To be condemnatory at this point would be hypocrisy for segregated evangelicals, but the two groups could struggle together with a common problem. The existence of the Black Muslims stands as a bitter reminder to white Christians of their failure for social justice as they speak of Christian love. Dialogue with the "Muslims" could afford an open valve of release of collective anger and as a summons to overdue repentance.

The possible levels of dialogue are at least the following:

1. The home—with the open discussion between evangelicals and the cultist caller.

2. The scholarly—with professors from leading evangelical and alternative institutions of higher learning, e.g., Brigham Young University.

3. The church—with lay involvement.

4. The community—with multi-church representatives responding to demands of, e.g., the Black Muslims.

There are few established patterns in evangelical-cult relations. These models can be established by doing. The basic requirements are an openness to persons and a willingness to grow. The alternative is for both camps to go unchallenged in partial understanding of God and man.

Christian discipleship, as defined in the Introduction to this book, involves ministering in this present world. This present world includes multitudes who have chosen to ignore or neglect the general biblical picture of Christ as Lord. Cultivating them to the degree of allowing the Holy Spirit to speak and convict is a part of evangelical responsibility to this age. The reward can be finding self in relation to God and those who search for him.

Appendix to Chapter I

There are at least ninety identifiable splinter groups within Mormonism, including the Cutlerites and Bickertonites. One of these groups is larger than the rest combined and deserves special attention here, especially because of a shift in direction the group is taking. Commonly referred to as the RLDS, the Reorganized Church of Jesus Christ of Latter-Day Saints has its headquarters in Independence, Missouri. Graceland College in Lamoni, Iowa, is under RLDS auspices. Currently the group numbers almost a quarter of a million in 1,100 congregations. Outstanding missions include a large force in Mexico.

The Reorganized Church started in Nauvoo when an argument arose over the selection of a successor to Joseph Smith, Jr. His wife, Emma Hale Smith, a strong woman, insisted that her husband had laid hands on Joseph Smith III, their eldest son, to signify his right to lead the church. She also claimed that her husband was not a polygamist, having married only her. When the majority chose Brigham Young, she and a small group of followers gradually migrated back to Zion in Independence, Missouri. The current president is William Wallace Smith, a son of Joseph Smith III.

There is little an evangelical Christian would object to in a newly-released "Statement of Faith and Belief of the Reorganized Church of Jesus Christ of Latter-Day Saints." Paragraph 8 contains a reference to "laying on of hands" as essential for salvation. An oblique reference to "Zion" in paragraph 12 does not tell all, including the view that Zion will be and is in America. Equally as important, however, is what is not said, including the issue of the *Book of Mormon*. In a pamphlet entitled, "Authority in Religion," and published by the RLDS press, the author states, "We believe that the 'everlasting gospel' was restored to earth in America in the year 1830. With it came the authority to represent God."[1] Another pamphlet makes the issue even clearer, "God, being an unchangable God and no respecter of persons, presents the same teachings as are found in the Bible, and in many instances they are made more plain."[2]

115

Regarding salvation, the RLDS group stresses Hebrews 6:1–3 as containing six fundamentals of faith: faith, repentance, baptisms, laying on of hands, the resurrection of the dead and of eternal judgment.

The RLDS group dislikes the label "Mormon." There are some chief differences with the Utah group of Mormons. The Reorganized Saints do not accept the *Book of Abraham* as divine. They maintain that Joseph Smith, Jr., never practiced polygamy. They are ruled by a prophet-president. The RLDS tithing system is that of one tenth given initially and another 10 percent out of total profit computed at the end of the year.

Just as important as the official differences between the Utah Mormons and the RLDS is the shift in direction by RLDS leaders. The RLDS group petitioned for associate membership in the National Council of Churches in 1968 and was accepted. The trend is more toward making the RLDS beliefs and practices acceptable to mainstream Protestantism. This was very evident in a conversation this author had in 1971 with Clifford A. Cole, president of the Council of Twelve Apostles of the RLDS group. Mr. Cole indicated frequently how the group was changing, largely because of the prophetic nature of the church. He attributed the change to the guidance of the Holy Spirit. An outside observer might notice that RLDS leadership is becoming more theologically aware in this process of syncretism of thought. For example, Mr. Cole's training includes work at five major universities.

The Reorganized Church of Jesus Christ of Latter-Day Saints is changing. Hopefully, it will continue to move toward evangelical Christianity.

Notes

Introduction

1. "A Letter to the Aquarians," *National Catholic Reporter,* February 4, 1970, p. 8.
2. J. K. Van Baalen, *The Chaos of Cults* (Grand Rapids: Wm. B. Eerdmans Publishing Co., 1938).
3. *The Social Teaching of the Christian Churches* (New York: The Macmillan Co., 1931), Vol. I, p. 336.
4. *Christian Deviations* (Philadelphia: Westminster Press, 1965), p. 8.
5. *The Social Sources of Denominationalism* (New York: World Publishing Co., 1929), p. 19.
6. Davies, *op cit.,* p. 24.
7. *Sociology of Religion* (New York: Fordham University Press, 1967), Vol. II, p. 313.
8. Richard Mathison, *Faiths, Cults, and Sects of America* (New York: Bobbs-Merrill Co., 1960), p. 370.
9. "The Place of Feeling in Religious Awareness," *Canadian Journal of Theology,* October, 1968.

Chapter I

1. Marden J. Clark, "Some Implications of Human Freedom," *Dialogue,* Summer, 1970, p. 48.
2. O. Kendall White, "Transformation of Mormon Theology," *Ibid.,* p. 24.
3. *View of the Hebrews,* Second Edition, 1825, p. 223.
4. See Fawn M. Brodie, *No Man Knows My History* (New York: Alfred A. Knopf, 1966), p. 47.
5. Le Grand Richards, *A Marvelous Work and a Wonder* (Salt Lake City: Deseret Book Co., 1966), p. 1.
6. *Ibid.,* p. 41.
7. *Ibid.,* p. 150.
8. Joseph Fielding Smith, *Teachings of the Prophet Joseph Smith,* p. 345.
9. *Ibid.,* p. 340 f.
10. John J. Stewart, *The Glory of Mormonism* (Salt Lake City: Mercury Publishing Co., Inc., 1963), p. 239.
11. Alice Felt Tyler, *Freedom's Ferment* (New York: Harper, 1962).

Chapter II

1. "Working Hard for the Reward of Eternal Life," *The Atlanta Daily World,* July 27, 1971, p. 1.
2. "What Do Jehovah's Witnesses Believe?" a press release issued July 1, 1971, by Louis D. Smith.
3. *Let God Be True* (Brooklyn: Watch Tower Bible and Tract Society, Inc.), p. 108.
4. *Ibid.,* p. 40.
5. *Make Sure of All Things* (Brooklyn: Watch Tower Bible and Tract Society, Inc., 1952), p. 86.
6. *Ibid.*
7. *Let God Be True,* p. 106.

Chapter III

1. October, 1971, p. 45.
2. New York: Vantage Press, 1966, p. 16.
3. *Destiny,* Vol. XXXVI, No. 12, December, 1955, p. 275.
4. *Ibid.*
5. Herbert W. Armstrong, *The United States and British Commonwealth in Prophecy* (Pasadena: Ambassador College Press, 1967), p. 20.
6. *Ibid.,* p. 211.
7. M. H. Gayer, *The Heritage of the Anglo-Saxon Race* (London: M. H. Gayer, 1928), p. 28.
8. *Ibid.,* p. 92.
9. Armstrong, *The United States* . . . , *op. cit.,* p. 1.
10. Gayer, *op cit,* p. 139.
11. April, 1967, p. 4.
12. Gayer, *op. cit.,* p. 47.
13. Herbert W. and Garner Ted Armstrong, "The Wonderful World Tomorrow," p. 30.
14. Herbert W. Armstrong, "1975 in Prophecy," p. 16.
15. *Ibid.,* p. 24.
16. "The Wonderful . . . ," *op. cit.,* p. 56.
17. "1975 in Prophecy," p. 56.
18. April, 1967, p. 9.
19. *Ibid.*
20. "The Wonderful . . . ," p. 35.
21. Herbert W. Armstrong, "Does God Heal Today?" (Pasadena: Ambassador College Press, 1952).
22. Herbert W. Armstrong, "Is Water Baptism Essential?" *The Plain Truth,* June, 1967.
23. *"The United States* . . . ," *op. cit.,* pp. 17–18.
24. William F. Dankenbring, "The Coming Control of Life," *The Plain Truth,* September, 1971, p. 27.

Chapter IV

1. *Science and Health with Key to the Scriptures* (Boston: Published by the trustees under the will of Mary Baker G. Eddy, 1875), p. 354.

2. Adapted from Charles S. Braden, *Spirits in Rebellion* (Dallas: SMU Press, 1963), p. 10.

3. "Unity School of Christianity" (Lee's Summit, Missouri: Unity School of Christianity, 1969), p. 9.

4. *Wee Wisdom,* February, 1971, p. 23.

5. Duane Valentry, "Show Business and Christianity Can Go Together," *New,* February, 1970, p. 8.

6. Bernard Dozier, "This Is Unity!" (Lee's Summit, Missouri: Unity School of Christianity, 1969).

7. "What Unity Teaches" (Lee's Summit, Missouri: Unity School of Christianity, 1966), p. 3.

8. See Horation W. Dresser, *The Quimby Manuscripts* (New York: T. Y. Crowell, 1921).

9. *Saturday Review,* January 13, 1968, p. 86.

10. Charles S. Braden, *Christian Science Today* (Dallas: SMU Press, 1958), p. 31.

11. *Science and Health, op. cit.,* p. vii.

12. *Ibid.,* p. 146.

13. *Ibid.,* p. 183.

14. *Ibid.,* p. 185.

15. From William L. Hendricks, *The Cults* (Fort Worth: Southwestern Baptist Theological Seminary, 1963), p. 57.

16. Mary Baker G. Eddy, *Retrospection and Introspection* (Boston: Published by the trustees under the will of Mary Baker Eddy, 1920), p. 70.

17. *Science and Health,* p. 466.

18. *Ibid.,* p. 242.

19. Mary Baker G. Eddy, *Miscellaneous Writings* (Boston: Published by the trustees under the will of Mary Baker Eddy, 1897), p. 261.

20. *Science and Health, op. cit.,* p. 331.

21. *Ibid.,* p. 336.

22. *Ibid.,* p. 350.

23. *Miscellaneous Writings,* p. 170.

24. *Science and Health, op. cit.,* p. 55.

25. *Ibid.,* p. 475.

26. *Ibid.,* p. 415.

Chapter V

1. Gayraud S. Wilmore, "From Protest to Self-Development?" *Trends,* December, 1971, p. 9.

2. Bernard Cushmeer, "Bible Tells Coming of the Messenger," *Muhammad Speaks* (Chicago) Vol. 35, p. 25.

3. *Black Muslims in America* (Boston: Beacon Press, 1961), p. 108.

4. *Ibid.*, p. 15.

5. *Ibid.*, p. 195.

6. *Muhammad Speaks*, XI, 1, January 7, 1972, p. 40.

7. "The Hate That Hate Produced," a television documentary by Mike Wallace and Louis Lamax, *Newsbeat* (New York: WNTA-TV, July 10, 1959).

8. "Mr. Muhammad Speaks," *Pittsburg Courier,* May 2, 1959.

9. Note: This date was borrowed from the Jehovah's Witnesses. W. D. Farad urged his early followers to read the writings of "Judge" Rutherford, the leader of that group in the 1930's.

10. P. 13.

11. "Mr. Muhammad Speaks," *op. cit.*

12. Lincoln, *op. cit.*, p. 220.

13. "The Black Wasps," *Trans-Action,* May, 1969, pp. 8–9.

14. Elijah Muhammad, "Hate Teaching," *Muhammad Speaks,* May 9, 1969, p. 21.

15. Lincoln, *op. cit.*, p. 27.

16. "What the Muslims Want," *Muhammad Speaks,* January 14, 1972, p. 40.

17. Dwight Cashimere, "Land in the Black Belt of Alabama," *Muhammad Speaks,* May 16, 1969, pp. 5–6.

18. Lincoln, *op. cit.*, pp. 24–26.

19. *Ibid.*, p. 222.

Chapter VI

1. *Wind Bell,* Fall, 1968, p. 27.

2. La Verne S. Sasaki, "Whither American Buddhism?" April, 1967, p. 1.

3. London: Luzac and Company, 1927.

4. Huston Smith, *The Religions of Man* (New York: Harper & Row, 1965), p. 95.

5. Vivekananda, *The Complete Works* (Almora: Advaita Ashrama, 1924–32), Vol. III, pp. 276 f.

6. Vivekananda, *The Yoga and Other Works* (New York: Ramakrishna-Vivekananda Center, 1953), p. 1.

7. See Edmund D. Soper, *The Inevitable Choice* (New York: Abingdon Press, 1957), p. 13.

8. Martin Ebon, ed., *Maharishi the Guru* (New York: Signet Books, 1967), p. 23.

9. *Ibid.*, p. 43.

10. *Back to Godhead,* No. 39, p. 3.

11. *Christianity and World Religions* (Nashville: Convention Press, 1963), p. 135.
12. *Christianity in World Perspective* (New York: Oxford University Press, 1968), p. 85.
13. *The Finality of Christ* (New York: Abingdon Press, 1966), p. 198.

Chapter VII

1. *Unitarian Christianity and Other Essays* (New York: The Liberal Arts Press, 1957), p. 3.
2. *Three Prophets of Religious Liberalism* (Boston: Beacon Press, 1961), p. 112.
3. *Ibid.,* p. 122.
4. Austin Phillip Hewett, *An Unfettered Faith* (London: The Lindsey Press, 1955), p. 51.
5. Channing, *op. cit.,* p. 87.
6. "Unitarians and Universalists Believe" (Boston: Unitarian Universalist Association, 1967), p. 1.
7. *Ibid.,* p. 3.
8. *Three Prophets, op. cit.,* p. 57.
9. Jack Mendelsohn, *Why I Am a Unitarian* (New York: Thomas Nelson and Sons, 1960), p. 192.
10. Hewett, *op. cit.,* p. 114.
11. *A Pocket Guide to Unitarianism* (Boston: Beacon Press, 1954), p. 5.
12. *Ibid.,* p. 48.
13. Quoted from Frank S. Mead, *Handbook of Denominations in the United States* (Nashville: Abingdon Press, 1951), p. 212.
14. *A Pocket Guide, op. cit.,* p. 7.
15. *A Place to Stand* (New York: Harper & Row, 1969), p. 36.
16. *A Pocket Guide, op. cit.,* p. 36.

Conclusion

1. *People Who Care* (Nashville: Broadman Press, 1967), p. 75.
2. *Let God Be True* (New York: Watchtower Society, 1952), p. 98.
3. *How the Church Can Minister to the World Without Losing Itself* (New York: Harper & Row, 1964), p. 81.
4. *New Directions in Theology Today.* Vol. I (Philadelphia: Westminster Press, 1966), p. 38.
5. *The Christian Doctrine of the Church, Faith, and the Consummation* (London: Lutterworth Press, 1962), p. 293.
6. *Ibid.,* p. 301.
7. *Op. cit.,* p. 21.

Appendix to Chapter I

1. Chris B. Hartshorn, "Authority in Religion" (Independence: Herald House, 1967), p. 5.

2. Myron F. La Pointe, "An Introduction to the Reorganized Church of Jesus Christ of Latter-Day Saints" (Independence: Herald House, 1967), p. 7.

Notes

Notes

Notes

Notes

Notes

Notes